Once a Parent
Always
a Parent

For a list of other books by

Stephen A. Bly

or information regarding

speaking engagements,

write or call:

Stephen Bly

Winchester, Idaho 83555

208-924-5885

Once a Parent
Always
a Parent

Stephen A. Bly

TYNDALE

Tyndale House Publishers, Wheaton, Illinois

ONCE A PARENT, ALWAYS A PARENT
Copyright © 1993 by Stephen Bly

Library of Congress Cataloging-in-Publication Data
Bly, Stephen A., 1944—
    Once a parent, always a parent / Stephen Bly.
        p.   cm.
    ISBN 1-56179-674-3
    1.   Parent and adult child.   I.   Title
  HQ755.86.B595   1993
  306.874–dc20
  93–4896

  CIP

A Focus on the Family book published by
Tyndale House Publishers, Wheaton, Illinois.

Unless otherwise noted, Scripture quotations are from the
New American Standard Bible, © 1960, 1962, 1963, 1968, 1971,
1973, 1975, 1977 by The Lockman Foundation.

Scripture quotations designated NIV are from the HOLY
BIBLE, NEW INTERNATIONAL VERSION®. Copyright ©
1973, 1978, 1984 by the International Bible Society. Used by
permission of Zondervan Publishing House. All rights
reserved.

Some people's names have been changed to protect the privacy of the individuals involved.

Editors: Lila Empson and Gwen Ellis
Cover Design: Candi Park D'Agnese
Interior Design: Tim Howard

Printed in the United States of America

99 00 01 02 03 04 / 10 9 8 7 6 5 4 3

for

Russell Stewart & Lois Margaret and

Michael Stephen & Michelle Dawn

Contents

CHAPTER 1

What Empty Nest?

And Other Surprises from Our Adult Children

IT WAS ALMOST MIDNIGHT.

I had been talking with our middle son, Michael, for five straight hours. He and his wife had driven twelve hundred miles to visit us. We had spent the evening discussing careers, working, giving your life to a vocation, and how to find some satisfaction and purpose in all of that. It was the kind of session fathers and 25-year-old sons should have.

We hadn't quite finished when the phone rang. A phone that rings that late seldom brings good news. This was no exception. It seemed that our oldest son's little boy, Zachery, had a stomachache and had been crying for hours. Russell and Lois were desperately seeking some experienced grandparental wisdom. My wife, Janet, and I spent a good half hour on the phone.

"Dad, we're really worn out," Russell reported. "Zach's been keeping us up night after night. We haven't slept much for days! I can hardly wait until my kids get older and I can get some rest!"

I don't know what I told him, but I remember exactly what I thought. *I can hardly wait until my kids get older so I can get some rest!*

From time to time, people come up to me at family seminars and say, "Thanks for speaking tonight, but we've already raised our kids!" They're right.

And they're wrong.

Sometime between the ages of 18 and 20 in our children, a dramatic turn of events takes place in our parenting. Dr. James Dobson calls it our "final release from parental responsibility"[1]; that is, we have completed the task of our responsibility for our children's day-to-day behavior.[2]

That is when we let them go. "We are given 18 or 20 years to interject the proper values and attitudes," Dobson says, "then we must take our hands off and trust in divine leadership to influence the outcome."[3]

The parental role changes drastically at this time, but it has not been eliminated. As long as we live, we will be much more to our children than simply friends, counselors, or encouragers. We will always be Mom and Dad. Neither distance nor neglect can break the bonds that tie us to them.

Our obligations to them change quite dramatically, however. Up to this point, we have interjected our parenting into their lives in decreasing levels of intensity. But from this point on we must stop altogether. The adult child must now be the one to determine when and where our love, wisdom, and skills are needed.

Very few adult children abandon their parents completely. From time to time, they will ask their parents to take up that responsibility again. And in that sense, because we will always be Mom and Dad, we will always be "parenting."

A closer look at the crowded nest reminds us of this truth.

No matter which secular childcare books we might have read since World War II, they all told us about the same thing. We were unanimously counseled that raising successful children would take intense parental care and concern for about 20 years. During that time, we were to teach them maturity, wisdom, and independence.

Little Junior would learn to control his temper. He would finely tune his motor skills. He would quit throwing sand at the neighbor girl. He would learn responsibility and money management from his paper route, teamwork from Little League, devotion to country and community through Scouts. He would learn about God in Sunday school. And discover sex from the clinical sixth-grade films. Then he would take college prep classes in high school, get a fine degree from the university, and in his senior year he would meet a charming young woman whom he'd marry, right after he was established in a nifty-paying job.

Then, like an eaglet stumbling from the aerie on its first flight, he would appear as a fully grown adult ready to take his impressive plunge into society.

This, of course, meant that parents were finally free from the tremendous emotional, economic, and social stresses of child raising, which, we were all assured, would allow us time to "do something for ourselves." To meet the need, a flood of activities was introduced by enterprising marketers. Something called adult education came along. Mothers who were not already in the work force were encouraged to start midlife careers. Travel trailers and motor homes cropped up in every other driveway.

"Your parenting hassles are over!" the books touted. "Go to Europe! Sail the Pacific! Build that mountain cabin! Purchase a car that doesn't have peanut butter permanently smeared on the backseat! Take up golf! Tennis! Bridge!" Or was it oil painting?

It doesn't matter.

The books didn't tell the whole story.

For many, the empty nest is a myth.

Jason lives down the street and drives one of the nicest Corvettes I've ever seen. It's a black '65 that he keeps shined to mirror perfection. Every Friday and Saturday night, he takes the 'vette into the city and cruises 21st Street. To maintain the expense of repairs, insurance, and general upkeep of such a rig, Jason works at odd jobs around town. He housesits, paints barns, and drives a truck during harvest.

Sounds like an industrious 17-year-old with expensive tastes, doesn't he?

But Jason is 31 years old and still lives at home with his parents, Matt and Sherry. He has attended seven different colleges, never more than a couple of months at each one. He's had great jobs, lousy jobs, but mostly no jobs. Matt pays the light bill, the house mortgage, and for groceries. Jason, when he has the money, pays for the cable TV.

Five times Jason has left home to begin an independent life; five times he has returned. Matt and Sherry sometimes feel resigned, sometimes angry, and sometimes like failures. Often they just feel trapped.

Trisha was a junior in college, living 900 miles from home, when she decided to get married—to a divorced man 10 years her senior. Her parents tried to persuade her to wait until after graduation. They warned her that it would be difficult. They cautioned her about dropping out of school. They described how tough life can be in the big city.

"Get to know him better."

"Wait until you see evidence of his religious faith."

"Don't make a mistake you will regret the rest of your life."

"We just don't want you to get hurt."

But the tingle of love and lust can defy logic. A cheap wedding band and a quick trip to Mexico marked Trisha's decision.

No more white four-poster in the front bedroom.

No more prom dresses mashed in the hall closet.

No more horse pictures thumbtacked to the ceiling.

No more Trisha.

The nest was empty.

Three years, two children, and countless bruises and black eyes later, Trisha and the kids took the Greyhound bus back to her parents' house. Dad now pays the bills, and Mom works at the insurance company until noon, then baby-sits the kids. Trisha returned to college and is working toward a teaching degree. She spends every day at school and every evening doing homework.

The nest is more than full, it's crowded.

The crowded nest is only one of the dilemmas that confront those of us who have adult children.

Whether our adult children live at home, across town, or across the country, we parents fill a unique role in their lives. Whenever we fill that role, we are still in the process of parenting.

William Saroyan entitled one of his last books *Sons Come & Go, Mothers Hang in Forever*.[4] He's right. Our roles will certainly change and vary with age and circumstances, but we will always be parents. And our job is never finished.

Since time began, folks have been parenting adult children. But it's only been the past 50 years that it's been seen as a "problem."

> The postwar model of parenting was one of heavy investment in children but with a time-limited commitment.[5]

> Influenced greatly by theorists like Spock, parenting became locked into developmental guidelines that suggested intensive support of children until young adulthood.[6]

> The role transitions of early adulthood, for example, include career choice, end of schooling, entry into marriage and parenthood, and establishing economic independence from parents.[7]

Parenting was seen as having a start and a finish. Sort of like a child's board game. If you had some bad breaks, you might have to slide back and repeat a section. But sooner or later we all make it to the finish line and everyone wins! The game is over.

We have been told by the secular experts that our parental role ends when our children are in their late teens or early 20s, and, for the most part, we accepted it as true. The prospect of the cessation of our parental role comes with a sugarcoating that appeals to our self-centeredness.

We were warned to expect a tremendous emotional crisis when the last child left home. To offset that strain, parents were told to focus energy, talent, and finances on themselves (who, it is implied, really deserve to have lives independent of their children).

It sounds ideal. But, in the real world, very few children—or their parents—continuously live "happily ever after."

Few parents nowadays complain about the crisis of an empty nest. Rather, they shudder at the thought that the nest will never become empty.

All around the country, I hear parents saying things such as:

"By now, I expected the kids to be grown and gone!"

"All our friends are taking cruises to the

Caribbean, and we've still got kids at home!"

"If we ever get this gang out on their own, we're going to buy a little condo on the golf course."

During this intensive but time-limited period of parenting, some people get the idea that children have rights and agendas that are separate from those of the family. Parents are portrayed as greedy, jealous, lusting, violent people waiting to steal fortune and virtue from the children.

The courts have shown increased interest in protecting the rights of children, even, at times, when it might be detrimental to the family. (For example: allowing children to have abortions without the consent of parents.)

There are certainly times when we need external intervention to protect the health, safety, and well-being of children. There is, however, a seldom-mentioned side effect from all of this—the separation of parent and child.

With so many sources telling us how independent children are supposed to become, no wonder it's a shock to some parents when they realize their involvement in their children's lives continues even when the kids are old enough to vote and drink.

My friend Sue summed it up this way:

> When Tami was three, I was told she would develop her social skills faster if I put her in

a preschool. When she was six, I drove her 30 miles twice a week for gymnastics to develop her confidence and balance. Then it was dance lessons, charm school, and the concert guitar. Educational television and Encyclopaedia Britannicas supplemented her education. I took her to a night class at the college during her senior year in high school to get a jump on calculus. A summer spent working in a third-world country was to teach her compassion and world concern. Her sorority was all she needed to know about friendships and commitment. One home economics elective taught her how to cook and balance a checkbook, and a psychology class prepared her for marriage.

Well, Tami's now 34 and hooked on pain pills. She has been refused visiting rights to her two darling daughters. She's living at home with us. Sometimes I don't know how to respond to her struggles. I mean, that child hasn't "needed" me since she was potty trained. All I had to do was drive her somewhere and wait outside to drive her home. Now, all of a sudden, I'm needed.

Sue's situation is not ideal, but it's real. And she is not alone. That's what this book's about:

real moms and dads,
real adult children,
none perfect,
and, at times, all in less-than-ideal situations.

For us, a real family means three sons, two daughters-in-law, and at least two grandchildren. From time to time, no matter what their age, we find we're still needed in our roles as Mom and Dad.

Sure, my son may be 25, but I'm still the one who is called out at midnight on a cold winter night when he runs out of gas. When the baby throws a tantrum on the fast-food restaurant floor, it's Grandma and Grandpa who get quizzed about child care. When the kids are $1,000 short on a down payment for a house, it's old Dad they turn to. When a loaded diaper gets flushed down the toilet, it's assumed I'll know what to do.

Erma Bombeck once mused, "One part of parenting never changes. It's a steady job that continues long after you have counted those precious little fingers and toes. It continues through slammed doors and I hate you's . . . lying about skipping school right on up to 'I'm bringing the wife and kids home to live.'"[8] Many of us with adult children know exactly what she means.

I prayed for Mike on and off all day. You see, he has this big job interview pending. Even though he's been married five years and lives 1,200 miles away, he's been on my mind.

But still, I wish I could be there. You see, I was there when we brought him home from that Coalinga hospital in February of 1967. I was there when he walked through the orange groves to attend kindergarten at Ivanhoe Elementary School. I was there when he got his driver's license at age 15. I was there, waiting up, when he came home from his first date. I wish I could be there like I was the day when he and Michelle said, "I do."

I was thrilled when I saw him win.

Devastated when I saw him lose.

Now he's in the real world facing another win-lose situation. I'm up in the bleachers holding my breath again, wondering if he will hit a line drive or an easy pop fly. So I wait and pray and hope.

I can't bat for him anymore. He's on his own. Yet, there is a union between us that forever ties our thoughts, feelings, and actions together.

Yep . . . two of my kids are grown. But there will still be times when they need Dad's words . . . wisdom . . . hands.

In that way, my parenting role will never end.

CHAPTER 2

The Crowded Nest

When Adult Children Live at Home

FORTY-SIX IS MUCH TOO YOUNG TO BE A WIDOW.

Lynda lost Jared to a car wreck almost seven years ago. After the accident, she secured a position teaching fourth graders while raising her teenagers. She figures she's adjusted about as well as she could. The kids are older now. Jack, her youngest, is a sophomore at New Mexico State University. Julie, her oldest, graduated from college and then worked for two years in Las Cruces. Last September she moved back home, and it's been nice company for Mom.

One Friday evening, Lynda trudged home from school carrying 32 carefully crafted journals that needed to be corrected by Monday morning. On her good days, when Lynda gets her hair to look stylish, when she wears an attractive new outfit, when she has on dark nylons and high heels, and when her makeup is just right, she considers herself an attractive lady. At those times she doesn't look a day over—say, 35. But this wasn't one of her good days. She looked all of her 46 years and felt 66.

Her new shoes were killing her feet, so she jammed on the ratty old "moose" slippers the kids had given her years ago. You know the type, with the moose head on the toes? Only neither head had any eyes left; one head had lost its nose, and the other its antlers. But, "Oh, my," she sighs, "they are comfortable."

Julie breezed in from work right after her mom. She reported that she had to hurry because her boss had fixed her up on a date with his son, an intern at the hospital. She had never met Barry. "But I saw his picture on Mr. Bowan's desk," Julie reported. "He's really a hunk, you know, for a doctor!"

The house felt cold, so Lynda pulled on her old, green sweater before rummaging in the refrigerator. The cottage cheese had turned bad, and as she turned to dump it into the disposal, she spilled the entire carton on the moose slippers.

She cleaned the floor, wondering what it would be like to be hurrying around for a date. Julie's shriek jolted her out of her daydreams.

"Mother, the toilet's flooding over! Come quick!"

Pulling on a tattered apron, Lynda hurried to the back of the house with a plunger in tow. In a few minutes, she had managed to splash water over the floor and in her hair, which now hung down in her face. In desperation, she called her neighbor.

"Char said she'd run right over with a new plunger," she reported to Julie.

"Mother, how come this happens just as I'm getting ready for a big date?" Julie cried.

"Is that a rhetorical question or do you honestly expect me to answer?" Lynda muttered as she left the room, plunger propped over her shoulder.

As she headed toward the garage to look for some drain cleaner, the front doorbell rang. Assuming it was Char, she yelled, "Come on in! I've been waiting for you!"

As the door swung open, Lynda looked up from her rotten-smelling moose slippers, ratty sweater, soaking-wet apron, and matted hair to see an extremely handsome young man staring at her with his mouth dropped open.

"Oh, no!" he gasped. "You're not Julie . . . are you?"

Lynda laughed all weekend.

"Never, never in my life have I ever seen such a dejected young man!" The next week, her daughter bought her a light blue sweatshirt that read, "I'm not Julie."

Yep, there are some good times when adult children live at home.

And some humor, too.

Even when it's unintended.

Although this whole situation has only begun to be addressed by sociologists, it has already developed a number of interesting acronyms. Maybe what you need at your house is PRI—you know, Premarital Residential Independence.[1]

Many parents face the dreaded affliction of RYAS—Returning Young Adult Syndrome.[2]

And then there's my favorite, ILYA. Some communities are littered with ILYAs—Incompletely-Launched Young Adults.[3]

Or, in terms you and I can understand, "The kids are still at home! What do I do now?" Or, "Help! Our kids have moved back!"

There Is Some Assistance for Those with a Crowded Nest

First, if you have adult children at home, relax. It's a common phenomenon.

> Recent data from the National Survey of Families and Households (NSFH) indicate that, among midlife parents (age 45-54) who have adult children, 45 percent have an adult child living at home.[4]

Second, if you have adult children at home, don't apologize about it. It's not necessarily a sign of failure. Successful parenting means that you have helped your children become the persons God wants them to be. The Bible says it this way: "Train up a child in the way he should go, even when he is old he will not depart from it."[5]

Success is not determined by economic good fortune, scholastic achievements, social popularity, or how rapidly or slowly children pull away from their parents.

Why Adult Children Come Home

In recent years, several social factors have contributed to the fact that more and more adult children live at home.

Economics

Are the good times supposed to last forever?

The post-World War II generation chose from abundant jobs readily available for those who were qualified. We grew up believing that if we graduated from college, there would always be a great job waiting. The post-Vietnam generation is learning otherwise.

There are no guarantees that high-paying job opportunities will perpetually increase. And what about salaries? It is no longer a given that children will invariably make more money than their parents.

In some fields, an overabundance of college graduates is applying for a limited number of job openings. This means employers can be selective and demand even more stringent training. That translates into graduate school, spiraling education costs, increased college indebtedness, doubled independent housing expenses, and more kids needing to stay with Mom and Dad . . . just a few more years.

One friend reported that her daughter's husband had to turn down three entry-level teaching positions because they couldn't afford to live in those cities. "The starting salary in one place was $25,000," she wrote. "But the average price of a modest home was $220,000, and rent for any decent place was $1,200 to $1,500 per month. They couldn't make it unless Katie worked, and that would mean postponing beginning their family even longer. They're living with us until they save up enough to pay first and last month's rent. Buying a home, even around here, seems out of the question!"

Marriage Deterioration

High divorce rates mean two homes must be provided where there was once only one. After years of living in a society where divorce is presented as an agreeable alternative to working through difficult situations, many adult children more quickly jump to divorce or separation as the best solution available. The results of turbulent, broken relationships lead adult children to seek a place that provides security, stability, and acceptance. The natural inclination is to go home.

Chuck has a good job with the phone company. But when Marci took little Charlie and left him, he felt aimless. Big alimony payments and a court battle over custody kept him fearful of scraping together more borrowed money to set up an independent household. So Chuck is living, for the time being, in the guest room his mom and dad built above their garage.

One of these days, he keeps saying, he'll get a place of his own. But neither Chuck nor his parents can see that day on the horizon.

The Push Toward Quality Careers

Only a few decades ago, most folks were satisfied with a job that paid the bills and provided stability. Now, such employment is touted as inferior. A job must be personally fulfilling. It must challenge the inner person. It must be an extension and expression of your own essence. It must lead to upward advancements. It must be exciting.

Careers like that are sometimes hard to find. Brett spent nine years driving a cement truck. The pay was great. He was a bachelor, and he found ways to spend every penny he earned. On his 27th birthday, he realized that he really wanted more out of life than driving a truck. So he got rid of the condo at the beach. He stopped taking vacations to Maui. He traded the brand-new pickup truck for a sturdy used one. He lives at home, and he's taking art classes at the university. If you ask Brett, he'll tell about someday having his own studio and gallery. If you talk to his folks, they'll tell you they don't have a clue how long Brett will be living with them.

The Comfort-of-Home-Factor

Let's face it. Some of us just might be reaping the rewards of our success. We worked hard to make our homes safe, comfortable, relaxed, enjoyable retreats for our children while they grew up in a rather frightening and hostile world. Now that they have reached adult age, some children are in no hurry to abandon the comfort of the world we have created for them.

We spent 20 years telling them:

"Don't talk to strangers";

"Come straight home";

"Don't let them cheat you";

"The streets are dangerous at night";

"Good girls don't go into places like that"; and

"You can't trust anybody nowadays."

Is it any wonder some of them are hesitant about jumping out of the nest!

Nels and Germaine worked hard for years to fix up the rather run-down Victorian home they inherited from her parents. The stately home sits on a hill that overlooks the city. By both of them working, taking inexpensive vacations, driving only one car, and doing without, they were able to turn the old place into a showcase. A few years back, they put in a swimming pool and built a one-room cabana next to it. It was sort of a minikitchen and game room with an attached bath.

Their son, Jensen, has been the produce manager at the supermarket for three years. He had supposedly been looking for his own place, but he can't seem to find anything that compares to the poolside cabana at home.

Chances are he never will.

Six Problems to Anticipate When Adult Children Return Home

1. Arguments.

"Because I'm the mother, and I say so, that's why!" doesn't end the discussion when children are 29 the way it did when they were nine. You may find yourself arguing over whether to watch "Murphy Brown" or the Cleveland Browns. You may argue over who's responsible for washing the sheets and who's going to pick up the grandchildren's toys in the living room. You may even argue about whether everyone should be in bed by 11:30 P.M.

Chances are, your pattern of settling differences with your adult children will be very similar to what it was when they were teenagers.

2. Increased need for privacy.

Big people take up more space than little people. If your children have been gone for a while, you have probably expanded to fill all the spaces they vacated. You went ahead and bought more furniture, turned Sissy's room into Mom's home office, and put a pool table in Junior's room or a whirlpool tub in the downstairs bath.

But now Bradley (or is it Bethany?) has moved back and brought his (or her) belongings. The garage has become a storage room and the patio a weight-lifting gym. The closets are crammed, and an extra adult wants to sit in the recliner every night.

Your child may be trying to redirect his life and find a new job, establish new relationships, and set new goals. Those are important matters that need serious "think time"—quiet, private moments.

But parents also need privacy. When kids are little, you can tuck them in bed early and have some time to yourselves. When they are 34, six-foot-three, and 220 pounds, you don't do much tucking.

Mom and Dad need time to talk.

They need a place to relax.

They need uninterrupted opportunities to build their love and friendship.

They need privacy.

They need it now.

If not now, when?

Later might be too late.

3. Continuing sibling rivalry.

Cain and Abel weren't ratty little 10-year-olds when their disagreement led to Abel's murder.[6]

If you have other children at home when an adult child moves back, you'll have an easier time at handling the crowded nest.[7] But there will be sibling rivalry. And there will be rivalry between your resident adult child and your nonresident adult children.

The twins were never much alike. Penny sold everything she owned and sailed off on an extended vacation in Mexico. Genny worked hard to pay for her little apartment and buy a car. Now Penny had to move back home and is scarfing down Mom and Dad's pot roast while Genny's getting by on a bowl of tomato soup at her own place. "It isn't fair!" she moans. "They just spoil her!"

4. Disagreement over finances.

There will be times when you don't agree on how to spend your money. And you'll have plenty of discussion on how your adult children spend (or don't spend) their money.

More people cost more.

When our son and daughter-in-law stayed with us for one month, our electric bill (which includes hot water for showers and laundry) increased by $60, our telephone bill by $30, and groceries by over $200. I didn't bother trying to determine extra auto expenses or wear and tear on belongings. It didn't matter. We were delighted to have them with us.

But extend that out for a year . . . two years . . . 10 years, and money can become a source of serious contention. If the resident adult child is employed, tension can arise over how much he or she should contribute to family expenses.

Many major blowouts are over minor items. Junior, who's living at home while he puts his marriage back together, becomes furious because Mom and Dad drank the rest of the Diet Cokes he purchased for himself.

5. Extra tension between Mom and Dad.

Parents seldom totally agree over what to do when an adult child wants to move back home. They might not agree on whether they should allow him to move back at all, and they probably have few agreements over what the rules should be once he does move back in. This holds true with an adult child who has never left home as well.

Social scientists say:

> Fathers' satisfaction was lower when the adult child had returned home after marital dissolution.[8]

They added that:

> The more highly educated fathers reported significantly higher level of disagreement and hostility with coresident children, lower frequency of enjoyable time, and lower satisfaction with the living arrangement.[9]

> Mothers reported significantly higher levels of private talks and especially enjoyable time with adult children than did fathers.[10]

Most often, it seems, fathers see resident adult children as some sort of failure, while mothers view them as kids who still need mothering. There will probably be a number of extra arguments between the parents over the adult child.

6. Serious strain in households with returning stepchildren and in single-parent households.

For many, the early years of conflict with stepchildren can be tolerated because parents hope for relief when stepchildren reach the age to seek independent residence.

But what if the stepchild doesn't move out?

Or what if he moves back home?

Fred never had anything in common with Sherry's son, Travis. But he learned to put up with partially rebuilt motorcycles on the front lawn; black-leather-jacketed buddies rummaging through the refrigerator; and tough-looking girls with embarrassing tattoos.

After Travis moved out on his own, it took three years to get the grass growing, remove the oil spots from the driveway, and get the neighbors to start speaking to them again. Then Fred came home from work one day to find that Sherry had invited "Travie" to move back home.

The stepparent situation often strains the marital relationship between Mom and Stepdad (or vice versa) to a breaking point. "He's your kid!" becomes the battle cry.

In a single-parent situation, a returning child can cause an emotional and financial burden almost too great to bear. Most often, children who return home to a single parent return to the mother.

Nancy's secretarial job provides a minimum lifestyle. Her one-bedroom apartment is her haven. Coming home tired, she still has to clean house and take care of other living needs. She spends some time studying computer manuals in order to keep up with changes in her field and struggles to regain her self-image and a feeling of worth.

Then 33-year-old Karrie showed up on her doorstep, without any money or place to stay. Now Nancy sleeps on the couch in the living room. And she picks up dirty towels her daughter leaves scattered in the bathroom before whirling out for another evening on the town. So far, Nancy has not yelled angry remarks at her daughter, but she's not sure how much longer she can hold it in.

With all the ready-made conflicts that can occur within a crowded nest, it might seem it is something to be avoided at all costs. But that isn't necessarily true. While always striving for the biblical goal of independence for our children, we can still enjoy the benefits that come along with the strain of having an adult child at home. And for most of us, the benefits outweigh the struggles.

> When asked how well the coresident living arrangement worked out for them, a full 70 percent of the parents indicated it worked out very well.[11]

Building the Family

Even though things may be going fine for you, there probably could be improvements. Following are the four main areas that assure a strengthened family, which includes resident adult children.

1. Talk more but don't yell.

There should be a regular channel of communication through which all household residents can express their thanks and air their gripes. Rather than wait for things to burst apart, parents should initiate the discussion.

Weekly family council meetings might be a forum for you. For instance, every Thursday night at 7:00, the whole family may sit down, turn off the television and stereo, and discuss how things are going. Any subject can be approached. And any suggestion offered. You can tell your adult daughter that it is her responsibility to scrub the bathroom fixtures in her bathroom. And she can add that she doesn't feel it's necessary to inform you where she is every minute of every day.

Talk about days off, vacations, phone bills, automobile use, credit cards, late-staying friends, suitable video movies, and other necessities of life.

But no yelling.

No insults.

Just open talk, with every member of the household getting a chance to state his ideas.

Universally, it seems, arguments that lead to yelling quickly lead to disintegration of the parent/adult child relationship.

A family council meeting might sound a tad hokey at first, but a solid commitment to such an activity will reap untold communicative riches.

2. Divide the tasks and expenses.

"When adult children remain or return home, parent and child must negotiate roles and responsibilities in the context of a shared household," say researchers.[12]

Jot down a list of recurring tasks needed to make the house function:

> washing clothes
> cooking
> cleaning (general)
> cleaning (room-by-room)
> washing car
> sweeping garage
> building fire
> taking out trash
> mowing lawn
> doing dishes
> changing linens
> feeding the horses.

On and on your list might go. You get the idea. Then, work through the entire list with your resident adult child until you all agree who will have primary responsibility for each one of the tasks.

It's good to name a backup person for each chore as well. For instance, if you agree that it's the mother's task to cook supper, then you might want to appoint the resident adult daughter as backup. This means that if Mom is gone next Tuesday night to a meeting, she, and everyone else, knows that the daughter is in charge of feeding the family.

Some of these things might seem petty and obvious, but it's unlikely that many families often discuss such items, and it is the little things that can cause the problems.

If the delegation of jobs does not seem fair, it needs to be sincerely discussed and the chore list updated at a family council meeting.

3. Plan together where all of this is leading.

The biblical goal for this relationship was established early in the history of mankind: "For this cause a man shall leave his father and his mother, and shall cleave to his wife; and they shall become one flesh."[13] It is important to discuss what the long-term goals might be for the present living condition. Here are some questions to consider:

- Is your adult child going to stay at home until marriage or remarriage?
- Is there an educational goal to complete?
- Will your child need a job that pays a certain amount before being able to leave?
- Will your child set up an independent residence only when you have enough income to establish it?
- How will everyone know when it's time for your child to move on?
- Will it be acceptable for you to leave the whole matter open-ended or permanent?

Having a plan does not guarantee it will be completed. But it does unite all parties in a common goal. You are working toward the same conclusion.

Plans do change.

You thought your son was moving back home so he could finish college, but he then dropped out and spends his time tinkering in the garage, saying that he's working on a new invention that will make millions.

So . . . keep talking about those new plans until they become clear. Make sure your children are aware of their own plans and goals. You might need to tell Junior he will have to finish his college courses by next fall, because that's when Mom (or Dad) is planning to go back to school.

4. Spend time playing together.

How do you play with a 29-year-old son?

Find a way.

> Coresident parents and adult children must also negotiate their social interaction, the degree of shared leisure time. Parental satisfaction with coresidence appears to be highest when parents are involved with adult children in pleasurable activities.[14]

Maybe this would be a good year to sell the boat and buy season tickets at Dodger Stadium. Then you and your adult son could spend many nights at the park.

Or maybe it's time to sell your season tickets at the stadium and buy a boat so you and your adult daughter could water-ski at the lake.

Maybe there's a play, a concert, a film, a sporting event, an opera, a swap meet, an auction, a garage sale, a mall opening, a hobby, a vacation, a board game, a television show, a book series, a volunteer charity work, a rodeo, or a sunset to watch that will bring joy to both you and your adult child.

You come from different generations, but you live in the same world. Don't allow your home to be a lonely place, merely a room and a bed, for your resident adult child.

"But," you may protest, "aren't there times to say no to my adult children? Aren't there times to boot them out? Aren't there times to refuse to let them come home?"

Yep.

But not many.

Chapter 6 discusses in some detail how to say no, but several factors need to be noted here with regard to refusing grown children residency in your home.

You might have to say no if your resident adult child:

- refuses to recognize your authority over the home.
- is physically abusive.
- is verbally destructive.
- is using your home merely to avoid facing an unresolved situation (such as marriage difficulties).
- abuses or is addicted to drugs or alcohol and refuses treatment.
- repeatedly steals or destroys your belongings.

There are certainly other extreme cases. But they are the exceptions, not the rule. Search for reasons to accept your children, not for reasons to exclude them.

Jesus, in His legendary style of teaching, told the story of the welcome home given to the prodigal son.[15] The son (today we'd call him an Incompletely-Launched Young Adult [ILYA]) was portrayed in a worst-case scenario of taking his inheritance and squandering it on sinful pleasures.

Finally he dragged himself home, tail between legs, only to be welcomed back and reinstated in the family.

"But," you protest, "that son repented of his former actions!"

True.

But the dad didn't know that when he welcomed him back: "But while he was still a long way off, his father saw him and was filled with compassion for him; he ran to his son, threw his arms around him and kissed him."[16] Only then did the prodigal confess his failures.

There simply aren't many reasons to say no to your adult child needing residence.[17]

The empty nest?

I don't expect it to ever totally happen in our house.

At the time of this writing,

Russell is 29,

Michael is 26,

Aaron is 13.

It might be 10 more years before Aaron leaves

the house. That will mean 39 years of uninterrupted child raising in our home.

But our grandchildren live right next door. They are little now and need help coming through the snow to Grandma and Grandpa's house. Ten years from now, they will be quite mature and ready to spend lots of time with us.

I wouldn't want it any other way.
My vote is *for* the crowded nest.
It's a crisis with which we can deal.
After all, we're human, not birds.

Marrying Them Off

Without Letting It Drive You to Tears

IF YOU NEVER THOUGHT ABOUT YOUR CHILD AS AN adult before, you will. Just wait until your son or daughter stands at the altar, pledging vows to some total stranger whom you've only known for 10 days . . . or 10 months . . . or 10 years. That's why there are tears in your eyes. He's not the baby anymore. She's not Daddy's little girl. And you are certainly not the focus of your grown-up child's attention. It's not just mothers who cry at weddings.

Eight minutes after our first son, Russell, was born, I had his life planned. He would be an attractive, bright, truthful, caring little fellow who loved Mom, sports, ranching, school, politics, and the Los Angeles Dodgers. He would wear jeans, tennis shoes, and, in time, cowboy boots.[1]

He would be a good student, popular, and healthy. At 18, he would graduate from high school and attend a prestigious university on an academic scholarship. (Since MIT was so far away, I opted for Cal Tech or Stanford.)

After college (and perhaps graduate school), he would be successful in a profession of his choice (you know, mathematics, medicine, law, aerospace, architecture, or agriculture).

He would then meet a charming, delightful, witty, supportive, nonsmoking young lady who would be thrilled to become his wife. My first grandchild would be a boy who would, of course, idolize his grandfather. Now, at that point my dream faded. My work would be finished.

That was all around 30 years ago. And as I say, it took about eight minutes . . . tops.

When our second son, Michael, was born three years later, it took me even less time to plan his life. I merely made some slight changes in the previous plan.

To my surprise, everything did not happen according to my plan.

The first major change happened in the fall of 1967 when my wife and I received Christ as Lord and Savior of our lives. As I matured in faith, I began to realize that God might have some plans of

His own for my sons. So I added a couple of items to the boys' future: They would one day make a commitment to Christ and find mates who were also Christians.

At first almost everything went according to plan—until Russell turned 19. He had spent the summer working at a Christian conference center. When he returned home around the first of September, he asked if he could put off college for a while.

"I'd really like to take a break from school," he reasoned.

"Wait a minute," I protested. "That's not in the plans!"

"Whose plans?" he asked.

"Well, uh . . . you know . . . my plans . . . I mean, your mother's and my plans for your life." Then, with my best pious language, I asked, "Are you sure the Lord wants this?"

"Nope," Russell replied. "I have no idea what He wants. I thought maybe a year of work would help me sort things through."

I gathered up all my dreams and plans for this kid, plus my study Bible and an exhaustive concordance, and closeted myself in my study to discover what the Lord's will in this matter might be.

As I expected, I couldn't find one word in Scripture stating that children must go to college. In fact, I couldn't even find a verse that said parents automatically know better than 19-year-olds what is best for their lives.

Sure, I could attempt to club this six-foot-two-inch, 200-pound kid with fatherly authority. But somehow such pressure at his age didn't seem like the proper motivation for educational advancement.

I knew Russell would comply if we insisted. But I found I couldn't insist. I suppose I never could convince myself that it made all that much difference.

So I changed my plans for Russell's life.

Just a small delay, actually. All of the essential ingredients were still in place. I'd just have to wait a year longer for him to go to college. No big deal, I reasoned.

The big deal arrived the following summer. Russ returned to the staff at the conference center. Once again we made plans for college in September.

By the end of June, however, Russ called home to announce that he'd met a special girl.

By the middle of July, he was asking questions like, "Dad, how do you know when you've found the one?"

On August 2, he told us that he was thinking about asking Lois to marry him.

By August 6, we were taking the seven-hour drive up the coast to check out, firsthand, this flaming romance.

"Marriage!" I fumed to my wife. "The kid will barely be 20. What does he know about marriage? He needs to grow up. He needs to mature. He needs to, you know—"

"Find a steady job?" Janet suggested.

"Yeah! How can he possibly support a wife while he's going to college?"

"Maybe he won't be going to school this fall," she replied.

"But . . . it's in the plans!" I insisted.

"Whose plans?" she demanded.

It was a good question. At what point should your children stop living out your plans for their lives and begin to discover their own?

Whatever age that translates to in your family, it is the moment that you begin the task of parenting an adult child.

One of the most common places where that parenting role crystallizes is in mate selection. Unless you happen to live in one of the increasingly scarce cultures where mate selection by parents is universally accepted, you will not be choosing your child's husband or wife.

That doesn't mean you can't offer advice. But preferably the advice should come before your daughter is flipping through the catalogs to select a bridal gown. Probably the best time to talk is someplace back in high school when there is no real contender in sight. But any time is better than no time.

Whether it's your 18-year-old daughter who still lives at home or a 35-year-old son who's been out on his own for years, the day will come when one asks, "How do you know for sure whom to marry?"

Mate Selection

Here are a few questions that will get a discussion rolling about mate selection with your adult child.

1. Does this person bring out your best behavior?
This should be true whether your child is 20 or 40.

It was a bit surprising when we first met Lois's parents. They went on and on about how much they enjoyed our son Russell. He was thoughtful and mature. He seemed to be so understanding with their daughter.

I kept thinking, *My kid? Are they talking about my kid?* My constant thought had been, *What does such a sweet young lady see in this guy?*

That's when it dawned on me that Lois had the ability to bring out the best in Russell, and her parents had been viewing that best behavior. To my surprise, later on I learned he had the same effect on her. It's not always that way.

2. Do you enjoy being around his/her relatives?

"How do you get along with her family?" I asked the young man.

"Uh . . . I just try to avoid them," he sputtered. "We never got along. Not even before we married."

"Didn't that worry you at the time?" I asked.

"Nah, I married Sandy, not her whole weird family!"

Man, did he ever have a bum idea! Someone should have told him you do, indeed, marry the whole eccentric family. A family with a mom and dad, siblings, grandparents, aunts, uncles, cousins, and distant relatives who only show up in the middle of the night demanding a place to stay and 50 bucks.

Mike's fiancée, Michelle, walked into our home, kicked off her boots, and flopped across the couch. Why, you would have thought she was at home!

She was.

Your adult children need to feel as comfortable with their prospective in-laws as they do at home.

Kim-Su was a beautiful Korean engaged to a very anglo young man named Jimmy. As I went through marriage counseling with them, I asked her, "How do you get along with Jimmy's folks?"

Suddenly Kim-Su beamed. "Jimmy's parents are the greatest! You know something really fantastic?

They always take my side if Jimmy and I have an argument. Jimmy's dad treats me like a daughter; he makes Jimmy toe the line. I love it!"

Kim-Su was ready to marry the whole family.

Does that mean she always agrees with her mother-in-law? No, but then she doesn't always agree with her mother, either.

3. Do you have compatible views on sex, money, and religion?

"I suppose you've talked a great deal about sex, money, and religion," I asked.

"Nah," the prospective groom said. "We always get into arguments, so we just avoid the topics altogether."

Avoid the topics?

Great!

That means they're planting time bombs in the marriage that will just wait to explode. In two weeks (or two years or 20 years), everyone will be surprised that they're having a major marriage problem.

Encourage your adult child to discuss the following questions with his or her future mate.

(You know, you can always copy these pages and hand them to your child, saying, "This guy says these are important things to discuss. What do you two think?")

- "What will be a loving way I can tell you I'm not interested in having sex?"
- "Without threatening your ego, how can I let you know I don't enjoy this particular sexual activity?"
- "How can I let you know that I'd really like to make love without sounding like a sex fiend?"
- "How much money am I allowed to spend without first checking with you?"
- "How will we decide which bills to pay first?"
- "Is there such a thing as my money and your money? If so, how is that determined?"
- "In your own words, describe what it means to be a Christian."
- "At what times will biblical truth take precedence over our own opinions?"
- "How do we decide where to attend worship? And how often?"

4. Can you love this person for a lifetime, even if he or she never changes?

Gerri complained bitterly that Phil's explosive anger was about to destroy their marriage. "Did this come on all of a sudden?" I asked.

"Oh, I've known about it for years. He was this

way before we got married, but, well, I thought I was just the one to change him."

Wrong.

Hopefully, all of us mature and develop our wisdom and self-control. But we have no guarantee of those changes. If you can't accept your prospective mate just as he or she is now, marriage will be a tough grind.

If one has only recently repented, the other has the right to wait a while before marriage in order to see if the changes are genuine.

5. Do you and your mate view each other as equals?

Gary was 36 and had been married twice before. Tina was 21 and had never been 50 miles from home. Gary paid child support for four children. Tina was an only child.

Gary now admits to marrying Tina because she looked terrific in low-cut gowns and bikinis. He liked to show her off to his friends. And Tina admits that she thought of Gary as a replacement for her father.

Gary dominated, degraded, and ridiculed. Tina submitted, whined, and cried. It was never a marriage between equals.

The roles of husband and wife are biblically balanced and culturally taught. But there is absolutely no room for inequality in the relationship. A husband is commanded to treat his wife "as a fellow-heir of the grace of life."[2]

What does that mean practically?

- The rules are the same for the husband and the wife.
- The opportunities are analogous.
- The finances are equally available.
- Each opinion has the same weight.
- No decisions will be made by brute physical strength or subtle manipulation but by open, honest discussion.

6. Is your prospective mate serious enough to make a long-term commitment?

Brad got a special waiver and dropped out of the Navy after only two years of a four-year term. He was working at C & R construction but quit to take a job selling appliances. Before the construction job, he had painted lines in parking lots, before that he worked at a wholesale nursery, and last summer he was assistant manager at the Burger Barn.

Brad spent a couple years at Bible school before he quit. He spent six months taking flying lessons so he could work at a missionary radio station in Alaska, but he lost interest in the program one lesson short of getting his license.

Now Brad wants to marry Renae, Dave and Shirley's daughter. They're a little worried about his ability to make long-term commitments.

They should be.

It would be a perfect situation for a two-year engagement.

Renae mentioned that idea to Brad, but he got quite upset. He figured sometime between the big Labor Day sale and the beginning of the Christmas shopping season would be best.

Renae told me, "I think my folks are probably right, but if I insist on waiting . . . well, what if I lose Brad?"

What if?

7. *Do you and your mate understand each other's goals?*

If your son gets transferred to McAllen, will his future wife be ready to quit her job and move to south Texas? And if she gets transferred to Yellowknife, N.W. Territories, will your son quit his job and move with her?

Is it all right with him if she happens to make more money than he does?

Is it all right with her?

Will he retire in 25 years?

Will she?

Do both really want to do what they are presently doing for the rest of their lives?

If not, how will they decide when it's time to change?

Trent is leaving his position on the county prosecutor's staff to move with his wife and two children to St. Paul. Why would he leave such a secure and challenging job? So that his wife, Rowdi, can get her M.B.A. degree.

Where will he work?

He hasn't decided yet.

Why the move?

"Before the kids came along—even before we were married—we were committed to Rowdi's getting her M.B.A. It's just taking us a little longer, that's all. It's really no big deal. I mean, we've been planning it all along."

Smart folks.

Real smart.

Am I saying that parents should be marriage counselors to their grown children?

Never formally.

But I guarantee your adult children will, at times, seek your advice. You can always be there with an idea or two to suggest.

When they ask, "How will I know which person to marry?" you should have a little more to respond with than, "Oh, you'll just know, Sweetie!"

Marriage is a lot more than the tingles.

A whole lot more.

Four Crucial Times to Talk to Your Adult Child about His Upcoming Marriage

1. It's time for discussion when you have reasonable concern about the mate selected.

The emphasis is on *reasonable*. You might not be crazy about his job or his hairstyle or his grammar or his country/western music or his politics or his choice of a bumper sticker on his pickup, but none of these things taken alone is sufficient for you to express concern about the marriage.

Is there ever a time for parents to discourage their child from marrying a specific person?

Definitely.

But not often.

It's appropriate to discourage the marriage if you feel convinced that your daughter will suffer physical abuse with a potential mate. Or if you feel that your son's fiancée's openly known promiscuity will be a continuing problem. Or if there's a substance abuse problem that both are merely ignoring. You should express your concerns openly with your child.

Most times, your role as parent is to make sure your child understands the difficulties ahead. You will not often advise against marriage. Rather, you will advise your child to enter the agreement with an honest look at the problems that will come.

Cheri was 20 and Chuck was 28. He had been previously married and had two children. But Chuck was a great guy. His wife had run off with another man, taken the children with her, and filed for divorce. Chuck had tried for three years to slow the proceedings. But the divorce was final. Then one day his former wife dropped the kids off at his place, and she hasn't been seen much since.

Chuck wanted to marry Cheri.

Both were Christians, serious about their faith.

Both were crazy about each other.

Both seemed mature enough for a lasting commitment.

Still, Cheri's parents worried. Finally, they talked straight out to their daughter.

"Remarriages are more difficult than first marriages."

"Child custody decisions are seldom easy and present possible future stress and trials."

"Eight years is a considerable age spread when you are so young."

"Well," Cheri huffed, "does this mean you don't want me to marry Chuck?"

"Nope. That's your decision. We just want to make sure you know what you're up against."

Cheri married Chuck eight years ago.

They're still married, but it hasn't been easy.

Chuck's kids are back with their mother, and Cheri and Chuck have two of their own. But Cheri is often bothered that so much child support goes to the other kids. It's hard for her to share her children's daddy with others. The visitation times are hectic, and there are still late-night phone calls from the first wife asking advice about the kids.

"Well," Cheri shrugged, "my folks told me it would be rough. I guess it's just a lot more strain than I imagined."

"If you could do it all over, what would you do differently?" I asked her.

"Oh . . . I'd still marry Chuck," she sighed, "but I'd get myself in better physical shape, because I'm just too run-down. I'd insist that Chuck and I get some good counseling on how to handle problems before they come up. And I'd also probably set more long-range goals—I unrealistically thought everything would be settled by now. And I'd probably listen a little more closely to my parents' advice. But, hey, don't tell them I told you that!"

If it looks like it will be a struggle, lovingly tell your child. But in the end, you must support his or her decision.

Here are five phrases you are advised never to use with your adult children about their marriage:

"I told you so!"

"If only you had listened to me, but oh, no—"

"Didn't I tell you to marry Brian? He's a doctor, you know."

"You're better off without the likes of him/her!"

"You got yourself in that fix, and you'll just have to figure a way out."

2. It's time for discussion when all your friends are asking why your adult child isn't married yet.

The jokes about a mother calling and asking, "When are you going to get married?" are proverbial. We spend the first 21 years telling kids they're too young to marry and the next 21 telling them that time is passing them by. Yet we know that if anyone is nagged into marriage by worried parents, that person's marriage has one of the weakest possible foundations.

Single adult children are just as delightful, fun, interesting, successful, and community-service oriented as married ones.

You don't have to teach people to run when a bear chases them. You don't have to teach them to smile when eating a hot fudge sundae. And you won't need to tell them it's time to get married.

They'll know.

So you might only need a short conversation with your adult child. But that conversation will be deeply appreciated.

"Listen, sometimes we joke around about trying to find you a husband [wife]. But really, we like you just the way you are. We couldn't be more proud of you or love you more if you were married!"

Is that it? A three-line conversation?

Yep.

I know dozens of people who would be thrilled and relieved to hear those words from their parents.

3. It's time for discussion when it's time to begin planning the wedding service.

Often, the first major argument between an adult daughter and her mother is about the wedding service.

Why?

Parents see it as the last big hurrah they can provide for their daughter. And she sees it as one of the first events in adult life that she gets to plan herself.

In the long run of life, it will be a more important day for the bride than it is for the parents, so let the bride plan the wedding service.

Here are three bits of wisdom you can openly share at this time:

- A wedding should be honorable before God and witnesses.

- A wedding should reflect the bride and groom's understanding of the nature of the commitment to be made.
- A wedding should include a lifetime vow. (See Matthew 19:6 for Jesus' words on the matter.)

With these exceptions, nearly everything else is up to one's individual design. Encourage your adult child to check with his or her minister before too many plans are made. Then sit back and enjoy watching your child make the plans.

Be ready to offer advice and help if asked. A good statement might be, "What can we do to help you?"

You do not need to decide:

- How many bridesmaids there should be.
- Which cousins should be the candlelighters.
- Where Uncle Harry's first wife should sit.
- If the solo should come before or after the vows.
- If the bridesmaids' dresses clash with the curtains in the sanctuary.
- If it will be too warm to hold the reception outside.

- If it's respectable to use the groom's old pickup for a getaway vehicle.
- If the pillow mints should be pink or teal green.

Some moms have been surprised at how little they actually had to do. "You know," Marjorie told me, "I didn't think Casey had her life together enough to be some man's wife. Then I watched her with all those wedding plans. She buzzed right through them like a general organizing her troops!"

4. It's time for discussion when your child is remarrying for the second (or more) time.

Let's say your son is 42. He, his wife, and three children live 1,200 miles away. On the day before Thanksgiving, he calls to tell you that he and his wife are getting a divorce. It's your first hint of any difficulty.

You're shocked . . . confused . . . a little hurt . . . and very worried, especially about your grand-daughters.

As he concludes the conversation, he says, "Don't worry about me, Mom. I'll do all right. Say, did I tell you about this lady friend of mine?"

Within six months the divorce is final, the girls are with their mother, and your son is married to a woman you hardly know at all. Is there anything you can do about the situation? Yes, and here are some suggestions:

- If you are asked, let him know that you think it would be best to wait a few years before remarriage—for his sake and especially his daughters' sakes.
- At the same time, lovingly let him know that you believe divorce is not what God has in mind for families but that you will certainly not stop loving him because of it.
- Let your former daughter-in-law know that you would like to remain friends with her and that you will always be ready to show love to your granddaughters.
- Let your granddaughters know that you have not become one bit less their grandparents than you were before.
- Let your son's new wife know that she (and her children, if any) will be treated like first-class members of the family.
- Let the whole family know that each one of them is continually in your prayers.

Being parents of adult children usually hits its highest intensity when your adult child marries. Things usually don't turn out the way you've spent the preceding 20 years imagining they would.

"Well," I told Janet, "by fall, this summer romance will have cooled and by spring they'll hardly remember each other."

But by spring, we were all standing at the front of the church, watching Russ and Lois repeat their vows. It has been a delight to watch their marriage and family grow ever since.

About three years after that wedding, I was again challenged as the parent of an adult child. This time it was Michael, our second son, who asked, "Dad . . . how does a guy know for sure whom he should marry?"

I was a little more prepared that time. Whatever I advised must have been encouraging, because Mike and Michelle have been married more than five years now.

Twice I planned out my sons' lives. Twice the Lord changed the plans. And twice, I have to admit, I've been delighted with the changes. But my stint at guiding adult children through the question of marriage isn't over.

Our third son, Aaron, was in the high school graduation class of 1998. I'm sure that in the year 2002, he will graduate summa cum laude from a major university and then begin his fabulous career. Sometime before '09, he will meet a Christian young lady with a sparkling personality, and they will marry and live happily ever after.

Of course, I've been wrong before.
After all, plans do change.
And that's why I'll need to be there.
It's why you'll need to be there for your kids, too.

CHAPTER 4

Do You Still Know Where Your Children Are?

How to "Worry" about Your Adult Kids in a Nice, Healthy Way

IT WAS A DRAMATIC PHOTO. A MOTHER AND DAUGHTER reunited after not seeing each other for 17 years. I scanned the article, expecting to find a human interest story about a baby given up for adoption, a wartime separation of family, or a domestic kidnapping by a revengeful father. But I discovered it was none of those.

Helen (63) and her daughter, Patti (38), had "sort of just drifted away and lost contact with each other," the newspaper reported.

Lost contact?

Drifted away?

From your own daughter?

From your mother?

My word! What did that mother do for 17 years? What went through her mind when she thought of her child? What about Christmas? Other holidays? What was she thinking of when her daughter's birthday rolled around?

I never did learn what really caused the estrangement. But the news did demonstrate that they were happy to be back together.

Do you know where your children are?

Joyce was surprised to get a picture postcard from her son, Ken. All it said was, "Mom, I liked Maui so much last summer that I moved here in January. I didn't know if you had my new address."

"New address?" Joyce moaned. "I didn't even know he went to Hawaii last summer, let alone that he'd moved there two months ago!"

Our son Russell and his family live right behind us. So I stepped over there last night to visit (mainly with the grandchildren). But no one was at home.

"Where could they be?" I mumbled. "They don't have any meetings tonight. And the babies need their rest. Where could they be?"

But how much should you, as parents, be aware of your adult children's comings and goings? Just enough to keep you as a constant factor in their routine family life. Knowing where they are every evening is being a pest. Your concern is the long-term mental, social, and spiritual health of the whole family. You will face busy seasons (both yours and theirs) where communication becomes difficult, yet those are the times you must make sure the contacts remain consistent.

Guidelines for Communication

Here are some guidelines you might want to follow.

1. Assume it is as much your responsibility as it is theirs to keep the friendship growing with your adult children.

"It's been almost four years since Robert and his family have come home to see us," Barbara reported.

"Where does he live?" I asked.

"Akron, Ohio," she said.

"I suppose that's about 2,500 miles away."

"Yes," she continued. "Those grandchildren will be grown before we see them again."

"When did you last go visit them?" I asked.

"Oh, we haven't ever gone back there. It's just too humid in the summer and icy in the winter. They have tornados there, and it's such a long drive. You know, I just don't like those long drives." I was thinking, *The road is the same distance no matter which direction you travel.*

Don't wait for your son or daughter to return the message you left on the answering machine. You need not wait for your adult child to answer the last letter you sent, nor insist that this year it's his or her turn to come visit you.

You can make the first move—and the second.

2. *Develop a communication routine with your adult children, and be careful about keeping it.*

Janet writes letters every Sunday afternoon. Marilyn calls her daughter every Thursday night at 9:00. Harvey and Nadine spend Thanksgiving with their son and Christmas with their daughter (rotating every year).

"It's like a family tradition," they report.

3. *Adapt the routine to best fit the individual needs of each child.*

Tony Garcia is single, lives in a little condo in Los Angeles, and has a job that flies him home to his folks in Denver several times a year. Teresa, his sister, lives in Seattle. She and her husband have three little ones under six. Mom and Pop Garcia drive to Seattle a couple times a year but have been to Los Angeles only once in the past two years. That's okay. The routine seems to fit them all well.

Here are some minimum standards for retaining healthy relationships with adult children:

- Face-to-face visits:

    If they live up to 60 miles away—once a month

If they live 61 to 240 miles away—four
times a year.

If they live 241 to 480 miles away—twice
a year.

If they live more than 480 miles away—
once a year.

- People-to-people phone calls:
  If it's a local call—once a week.
  If it's a long-distance call—twice a month.

- Long, newsy letter:
  If they live more than an hour away—
  once a month.

Here are 10 times to visit your adult children:

1. When they change vocations—jobs, positions, ownerships, or businesses.
2. When they participate in their favorite
   hobby, such as a big Model A club rally,
   tennis tournament, sky-diving competi-
   tion, or art show.
3. When they make their latest major purchase, such as a new house, horse, boat,
   swimming pool, pickup, piano, or stereo
   entertainment system.
4. When they receive achievements or
   awards. Be there when they get the

Teacher/Salesperson/Community Volunteer/Plumber/Writer/Bull Rider (or whatever) of the Year Award.

5. When they are seriously ill or have been involved in an accident.

6. When they experience failures and setbacks in their career, relationships, marriage, or finances.

7. When they have special performances or recitals. Mom and Dad have always been the two most important people in any audience. So be there when she sings the solo in the church Christmas program, or his band opens at the county fair, or they star in a local production of *Fiddler on the Roof.*

8. When it's an obvious holiday, such as a birthday, an anniversary, Thanksgiving, Christmas, or Mother's Day.

9. When important community activities are scheduled, such as the annual 4th of July parade, the Trout Festival, the Lincoln County Rodeo, or the Spring Flower Show.

10. When you just happen to be in the neighborhood. If you're driving to Florida, and they live in Georgia, then you're in the neighborhood. If you are going to the Northside Mall, and they live out on North Fairview, then you're in the neighborhood.

If your adult child has children, you multiply the above 10 reasons by the number of grandchildren in that family. You always have dozens of reasons to visit or call or write.

It may sound like you'll be spending every waking moment with your adult children. But despite the horror stories about nosy parents, the truth is, it rarely happens.

Marci is 45 years old. She's been married 24 years and lives 382 miles from her parents. In that time, she has had the lead in the community theater production a half-dozen times. She staged a one-woman art show at the courthouse. She was nominated to receive the Teacher of the Year Award twice at the high school. She hit black ice, totaled her car, and was hospitalalized for six days. She taught at three different schools. She coached a girls' volleyball team to a league championship. She graduated from a local university and received a master's degree, summa cum laude. And she and her husband worked for four years to build, by themselves, a big log house in the foothills on the west side of the city. Her two daughters graduated from high school; one is now married, and the other just won the county-wide talent contest.

But Marci's parents have not yet made it for a visit.

It's not just a tragedy, it's a crime.

Do you know where your adult children are?

"I'm 26 years old, have been out on my own for five years, and live 600 miles from my mom. I don't need to tell her what time I got home on Saturday morning or what I wore or whether I remembered to floss!" Angie groaned.

She's right.

So, what should you as parents be concerned about?

Health.

Safety.

Career satisfaction.

Self-image.

Friends.

Spiritual commitment.

Mate/children.

Showing You Care

Here are three things you can do to keep your children in your mind and lovingly show them your concern.

1. If you want to know where they are, make sure they know where you are!

- Double-check to see that they have the telephone number where you and your spouse work.

- When you head out for a weekend trip, give them a call and tell them where you're going (you can even leave the information on their answering machine).
- Send them an itinerary of your vacation (addresses and phone numbers if you have them).
- And in letters and notes, let them know your normal weekly routine (Tuesday night Bible study, Friday afternoon class at the college, Saturday morning volunteer work at the food bank).

In general, let them know the kinds of things that you would like to know about them.

2. Make a habit of writing everything down about your adult children and their families.

I was surprised to see my friend Darlene in the dentist's waiting room. We visited as we waited, and I asked her about her daughter, Rebecca, whom I had not seen in several years.

"Becky's living in Seattle now," she reported. "She's working at Nordstrom's for the summer but is trying to get into a design firm. She's got a big job interview on the—" she paused, rummaged through her purse, pulled out a small bifold calendar, glanced at a date, and then continued. "The interview is on the 14th at 10:00 A.M. We're all a little anxious about it. It seems like the perfect position for her."

"You keep track of her with a calendar?" I asked.

"This?" she laughed. "The kids call it Mom's Worry Calendar. This is just for the kids' activities. What with Lance in Texas, Jennifer at Wheaton, and Becky in Seattle, it's tough to remember all they are doing. So whenever I get a letter or talk with them on the phone, I write their upcoming events on my calendar.

"Every time I'm stuck in traffic or waiting for a dentist, I pull it out and review what's coming up for the kids. It's been the greatest thing, because I don't have to remember every date and time. And I use it to remind me to send them a card or let them know I'm thinking of them. For instance, I found a great coloring book I'm going to send to Becky before that interview."

"A coloring book? Becky must be 25 years old!" I remarked.

"When she was seven, there was a coloring book with instructions on how to design and color coordinate your own clothes. She literally wore the pages through. Well, the other day on the bargain rack, I saw the same coloring book! I'm going to make sure she gets it a day or two before the interview."

"She'll have a lot of fun with those memories," I commented.

"Yeah, I figure it's not a bad investment for $1.49."

A worry calendar?

Think of it as a calendar of family events. If any event is important enough for your adult child to tell you about, it's important enough to keep some kind of record.

I have a feeling that a coloring book won't improve Becky's credentials or help her break into the clothing design business. But it's going to remind a young lady living 350 miles from home that somebody cares, that she has a rooting section that is always on her side, that where she is today is permanently tied to a lifetime of memories. Maybe it produces just a twinge of peace, satisfaction, and self-confidence.

Who's to say how much that might help her interview?

3. Have a regular prayer time for your adult children.

- If you have the time, do it every day.
- If need be, once a week will work.
- Pray with your spouse, if at all possible.
- Pray for the specific needs of your children (and their families).

- Pray for the important things. In the long run of life, there is only one thing worth worrying about. "But the LORD answered and said to her, 'Martha, Martha, you are worried and bothered about so many things; but only a few things are necessary, really only one.'"[1]

  What is that one thing? The Bible says, "Thus says the LORD, 'Let not a wise man boast of his wisdom, and let not the mighty man boast of his might, let not a rich man boast of his riches; but let him who boasts boast of this, that he understands and knows Me.'"[2]

  If we followed this line of thinking, then we should spend only a little time concerned by our adult children's wisdom, strength, and riches and lots of time concerned about their personal knowledge of God. This is the most important thing you can do for them.

- Let your children know that you are praying. We had just finished lunch, and Suzanne asked me what time it was. "About 1:35," I replied. Then noticing the watch on her wrist, I asked, "Did your watch break?"

  "Oh, no. I just leave it on eastern time whenever I travel."

"Isn't that a little confusing?"

"At times, but Lawrence is stationed in California, and Lannie's doing her internship in Pennsylvania. You see, I have this deal with the kids. For years now I've prayed for them every day at 2:00 P.M. eastern time. No matter where they are, if it's 2:00 at home, they can always count on my prayers. It's a habit with me now. They don't ever outgrow the need for our prayers, do they?"

Ten Ways to Show You Care

1. Frame an old picture.

Dig out a classic old photo of your children when they were young. Have five-by-seven-inch prints made from it, write dates, names, and ages, then slip them into nice frames and mail them to your son(s)/daughter(s) on a holiday. It is guaranteed to be the best present received.

2. Ask advice.

Ask your children's advice in a field where you seldom ask advice. If your son in Tucson sells automobiles, of course you should ask him for input on your next car purchase. But this year ask him about politics. Who does he recommend for senator? governor? president? Chances are you've been talking for years about your ideas, so this time listen carefully to his suggestions.

3. Display a current photo.

Keep your children's most current photos in prominent places around the house. Even though you have their second-grade class pictures on the wall somewhere gathering dust, keep the latest ones out and around. If you don't have current ones, ask! Tell them it's no different from when they were in school. You still appreciate having a *yearly* picture.

Also send them a photo (labeled and dated on the back) of you at least once a year. How many photos do you have in the house of your own mother and father—I mean, a photo of Dad all by himself, and a photo of Mom all by herself? They're meager to nonexistent, right? Case proved.

4. Keep their treasures.

Even though you do something else with their rooms, don't do away with all their stuff. Three days after our oldest son, Russell, was married, his bedroom was converted to Janet's office. It was a shock for him to stop by the house and see the change.

"What happened to my room!" he shrieked.

"Your room?" his mother replied. "You don't live here anymore, remember?"

Keeping their rooms just the way they were

when they lived at home is a little bizarre. Chances are you have a lot better use for the space. But what about all those goodies? You know, the Scout uniforms, the high school scrapbooks, the model airplanes, the dolls and stuffed bears, the drawers of grade school achievement awards?

If your adult children can't accommodate their possessions now, sort out the obvious junk (the melted wax vase, 97 broken crayons, and 243 pieces to a 500-piece jigsaw puzzle) and throw it away. And if you have storage room, box, seal, label, and store the other treasures.

Someday—usually about the time your grandkids begin to grow up—your children will be delighted to dig through the box. They might say, "Mother, why on earth did you save all this junk!" But then they'll turn away so you don't see the tears and sheepishly ask to take about half the stuff with them.

5. Enjoy their friends.

Laura and Staci were inseparable in high school. They took the same classes, went out for the same sports, joined the same clubs, attended the same church youth group, and, at times, chased the same boy. They were the type who would call each other before school every day just to see what the other one was wearing.

It was no surprise to anyone that they decided

to go to the same college, room together, and start out with the same major. But paths do diverge. By their junior year, Staci found it best to transfer to another school in order to pursue a new course of study. Still there were hundreds of phone calls, holidays, and summers together.

When Laura married right after graduation, Staci was the maid of honor. Less than a year later, the roles were reversed. Staci and her husband remained in Fort Wayne, but Laura and her family moved to Atlanta. It was a sad parting, for they were more like sisters than friends.

But Laura's mom refused to let such a great friendship die. From time to time she invites Staci over for lunch. She sits with Staci's two darling little babies. She remembers birthdays and holidays with a card or a gift. And each time Laura comes home, it's Mom, Dad, and Staci who are waiting on the front porch.

"For 15 years there was nobody more important to Laura than Staci, and my daughter still needs a best friend she can count on."

6. Say "I love you."

Okay, so Junior is 41 years old, weighs 280 pounds, stands six-foot-six, and drives a logging truck in Alaska. The heart inside that big lug is the exact same heart inside the little boy who used to run to you in tears with a scratch on his knee. It's the same heart that broke and needed your comfort when Tuffy got run over by the neighbor. It's the same heart that was utterly crushed when Junior struck out in the bottom of the ninth during the championship high school baseball game. The packaging is different, but the heart's the same. He still needs your love.

The next time you see that grown-up kid, toss your arms around him, give him a big hug, and say, "Honey, I love you!"

7. Participate in their adventures.

You have your things.

Your children have their things.

Your thing is tennis.

Your daughter's is aerobics.

You like playing bridge.

She likes whitewater rafting.

You enjoy the quiet shops downtown.

She likes going to the mall in the suburbs.

You like attending a play at the college.

She likes front-row seats at a rock concert.

Keep searching for opportunities to participate in your children's things. Some of them you might not want to attend no matter what. Some of them they might not want to share. But there will be some things you can do together.

Ellen shocked her grown daughter when she

announced, "I'm going on a trail ride through the Grand Tetons this summer."

"Mother," Vanya groaned, "you don't even like riding horses!"

"I know," she nodded, "you're the expert in the family. I was hoping you'd go along and teach me how to ride."

Vanya did. And mother and daughter had a delightful, but somewhat sore, time. Next summer they plan to ride across the Sierra Nevadas just south of Yosemite.

8. Brag about them.

You used to put every picture your children ever drew on the refrigerator door. You were thrilled when they bleated their way through "Mary Had a Little Lamb" on the trumpet. And you were ecstatic when a blooper rolled between the second baseman's legs and Junior got his first T-ball hit.

So keep bragging about them. You are probably still the main audience.

My father died 17 years ago. I've written 1,000 articles and 30 books, but he never got to see one of them. It's a constant regret of mine. Just once I'd like to hand him a book of mine and say, "Hey, Dad, I wrote this. What do you think?" I get a feeling he'd fasten it to the refrigerator door.

Brag about your kids.

9. Show support.

Give your children extra support during their big challenges. Send them a gift or a card, call, or visit them when they look into a new job, move to another location, confront the boss, or struggle in their marriage.

Trevor called his mom and dad to report that he and Sammi Jo were having some real problems. "Listen," his mom replied, "why don't you two borrow the travel trailer and take off to the mountains for the weekend? We'd be delighted to have the kids stay with us!"

They did.

And it's become a quarterly habit for almost six years.

10. Don't let them get away with sin.

Here's the tough one. Little children sin. Adult children sin. And parents are never given the freedom to overlook sin. There is a right and a wrong way to live.

Think about these key principles when discussing your adult children's failures:

- We all have times when we need to be confronted for failing to live up to God's standards.[3]
- Rebuke your children with patience and instruction.[4]

- Let them know that you are by no means perfect, but that you do want to help them overcome their failing any way you can.[5]
- Don't make enemies of your adult children. The goal of confrontation is a loving, biblical lifestyle and relationship.[6]
- Make sure your response exhibits true wisdom. "But the wisdom from above is first pure, then peaceable, gentle, reasonable, full of mercy and good fruits, unwavering, without hypocrisy."[7]
- Take time to consider the exact words (and tone of voice) you use when speaking to them.[8]
- Once you have made your position clear, don't keep bringing up the subject. Pray that the Lord will remind them of their problem, but know that you are free to go on and love them with all your heart.

Do you know where your children are?

The next time you meet an old friend on the street . . . one you haven't seen in years . . . he will probably ask you three questions:

"How have you been?"

"How's your mate?"

"What's happening with your children?"

You should have a good reply to all three.

CHAPTER 5

The Family Bank

Lending Money without Going Broke

I CAN HARDLY WAIT UNTIL THE KIDS ARE OLD ENOUGH to be financially independent," Jack groaned at a men's Bible study.

"Well," I asked, "just how old is that?"

Thad, the old-timer in our group, quipped, "Mine are 48, 52, and 56—and they still aren't above needing a few bucks from old Dad!"

Jack and Thad's positions aren't unique.

Walter and Penny own a house just down the gravel road from ours. Actually, they live on a ranch several miles away. But they also own a house near us, even though they don't particularly want to own it. We live in an area of the country where real estate is not the best investment to make. People are financially strapped, and rents are low. It's fortunate when you can sell a house for the amount you paid for it.

So why do Walter and Penny own this unoccupied, three-bedroom home? Because it belonged to their son, Tad. In order for him to qualify for a loan, Walter and Penny put up some money. Then the mill where Tad worked shut down, and he was so broke that he decided to just walk away from his loan and start over in Seattle.

Walter and Penny are making the payments and paying taxes to avoid losing the several thousand dollars they put into the place. They don't want the house and are hoping to sell it someday and recoup their investment. It doesn't look too promising, and at times they wonder whether they did the right thing by lending money in the first place.

Tex and Bea have a big-screen television in their small retirement home. I asked them about it. "Oh, we didn't buy it," Tex reported. "Our son, Gary, bought the thing. Then the depression in the oil business hit, and Gary couldn't make the payments. We bought out his share and are paying it off."

"It's huge!" I exclaimed.

"Yeah, sometimes we think about pointing it out the window and calling it a drive-in theater. But

Gary needed the help, and it was a spur-of-the-moment solution."

"Sort of ridiculous in this little place," Bea added, "but it's hard to sit back and not help the kids."

"I own a little bit of Idaho, myself," Smokey Segal told me in Phoenix.

"How's that?" I questioned.

"Our daughter and her husband wanted to build a place in the hills behind Boise, but they had to own property to qualify for a loan. So we bought the property for them. It was a strain on the pocketbook for a while, but when I see pictures of the grandkids playing in the big old backyard, it's all worthwhile."

"What happened to your boat?" I asked Chet.

"Sold it last fall," he related. "Melanie landed a good job in Carson City. She had to move right away, so we sold the boat to pay for a moving truck . . . and for the first and last month's rent for her and the girls. It was our only way to get some quick cash. We had to do something, right?"

Yep, I think Chet was right.

But is that always the case?

What happens when the love of family and the love of money clash?

Most people will not say they love money, but they love what money will buy—including security, peace, comfort, and possessions. For most of us, these things were too hard to come by to give them up easily—even to our adult kids.

Before You Offer Financial Help

Here are some factors that can help you keep a clear head when you are considering whether to offer financial help to your adult children.

Get yourself in good financial shape first.

Your own disastrous economic conditions will leave you little base for helping anyone else. Very few of us will ever be wealthy, but we can aim for stability.

Some great resources for money management are:

> *Victory over Debt: Discovering Financial Freedom,* Larry Burkett (Chicago: Northfield Publishing, 1992). No matter what your financial status, this book will help.

> *How to Manage Your Money,* also by Larry Burkett (Chicago: Moody Press, 1991). This is a basic financial management workbook to guide you with biblical principles.

> *A Biblical Theology of Material Possessions,* Gene A. Getz (Chicago: Moody Press, 1990).

Protecting Your Income and Your Family's Future, William Brock Thoene (Minneapolis: Bethany House Publishers, 1989).

You don't have to be a financial genius to figure out some rules for yourself.

1. Always spend less money than you make. Sound simple? The federal government hasn't figured out how to do it.

2. Work toward having a base for major financial emergency situations. This might include a savings account, home equity, a life insurance policy, or assets that can be quickly sold.

3. Almost never loan money you can't afford to live without.

I wanted to say *never* for number three. But then I thought of J. T. and his wife, Margaret, living in that 18-foot travel home for more than three years. They surely couldn't afford a $51,000 loan to their kids. So they sold their house and moved into the tiny trailer.

Their granddaughter, Shelly, had run up $400,000 worth of hospital bills during six surgeries and several months in the hospital. The family's share, even after the insurance settlement, was $51,000, so the house was sold to pay the bill.

"We'll pay you back somehow, someday," their son and daughter-in-law promised.

J. T. and Margaret aren't holding their breath. "We wouldn't hesitate to do it all over again," they report. "There are some things that just have to be done."

Distinguish clearly between gifts and loans.

Gifts should be gifts with no strings attached and no payments due. You can give the recipients your vast wisdom about investing the gift, but it's all theirs.

When Stan and Leona sold their farm several years ago, they took half the money and set up some retirement investments that would provide them with a continuing income. The other half they divided and made one-time gifts to their two children.

"The kids need the money more now than after we're gone. Besides, this way we get to see them enjoy it."

Their older child, Patrick, bought part interest in a sporting goods store where he had worked for years. The younger, Carrie, bought a red sports car, took a four-week vacation in Mexico, and invested the rest in gold coins. At the time, Stan and Leona sorely wished Carrie had used the funds more wisely. "Maybe we should have insisted she use the money for something else," they moaned.

Then last year she married the young man who owns the local coin/stamp/sports card shop and who sold her the gold coins. He's a great guy who's crazy about her, and they're expecting their first child in the fall.

"In the long run," Stan shrugs, "who's to say which was the best investment?"

When your kids ask, "Can you help out with a few bucks?" everyone needs to be clear whether it will be a gift or a loan. It is extremely important that everyone understands the arrangement.

Put all loans over $100 in writing.

Loans should be put on paper. Actually, you can set whatever minimum figure you'd like. Maybe in your economic condition, you need it in writing if it's over $20. Or perhaps it's no big deal to you until it's over $1,000. The point is, loans should be based on more than just memory.

Some transitions, family structure, and amount of loans might be so complicated that only an attorney can properly set them in writing. If that's your case, then get a lawyer.

But many times the sum or the situation is simple, and an easy, simple loan form can be drawn up (or even purchased at an office supply store).

Here are some elements you will want to include:

- Current date
- Exact amount of the loan

- Name(s) and address of the borrower(s)
- Name(s) and address of the lender(s)
- Rate of interest
- How the interest is to be computed (e.g., annually)
- How often payments on interest and principal will be paid (monthly? yearly?)
- Exact amount of the payments
- Date the first payment is due
- Date the last payment will be given
- Some legal-sounding line that states the interest will be paid first (as each payment is made it shall be applied first in payment of the interest then due, and the remainder on account of the principal sum, and thereupon interest shall cease upon the amount so paid on the principal sum)
- Any other conditions that are attached to the loan (e.g., upon the sale of the property at 123 Main Street by the borrower, the balance of the loan, minus interest due at the time, will be paid in full)
- What kind of grace period will be given for late payments, and what will happen if payments cannot be or are not made (optional)
- Place for borrower(s) and lender(s) to sign and date

It's really not complicated, and a clear document eliminates lots of misunderstanding.

Yearly, the lender should send to the borrower a statement listing how much money was paid on the loan during the year, how much went to interest, and how much went to principal. This can be secured from your banker, a friend at a real estate office, or various computer programs.

"Will all of that hold up in court?" you may ask. If taking your child to court is a very real possibility, then by all means hire an attorney in the first place. In our particular family, we find the idea so repugnant that no further documentation is needed.

Make sure you and your mate completely agree.
Agreement in parenting is an extremely important factor whether your kids are five or 50.[1]

If you throw in a mother's built-in closeness to her sons, a father's protection for his daughters, and then add a blended family, anything less than an explosion of personalities is a miracle.

Here are a few guidelines:

- Don't do it until you and your spouse completely agree.
- Don't do it if it has the potential for causing sibling contempt.

- Don't call it a loan if you both know your children can't possibly repay the money.
- Conduct all your discussions about the financial loan or gift in private with your mate.
- Pray together about the situation, and wait until you both feel spiritually at ease about the decision.
- Carry out the transaction with joy, releasing the results to the Lord.

Make sure everyone understands the strings that might be attached.

Maybe there's a lien on additional property.

Perhaps there's an agreement to pay off at the time of resale.

Maybe the loan is only for use in the home state. Maybe it can only be used for appreciating items.

Maybe if your children graduate from medical school or earn an advanced degree, you'll forgive the debt.

Don't feel as if you always have to give or loan your children what they ask for. The next chapter deals with saying no to your adults kids. And it just might be that loaning them money is, for you, one of those times.

Look for other ways to help.

When you just don't have money to spare, or when you think assisting with money is the wrong thing to do, help your children find another solution.

Avery and Carmen couldn't help the kids buy a second car. There just wasn't any money. But Avery lent his son the old pickup to use until they could save up for a down payment.

Tom's son, Chad, wanted to borrow some funds to add on another bedroom. But Tom knew that his son just couldn't afford any more payments, so he and Chad took two weeks off and built the room themselves, saving about 60 percent of the estimated cost.

Chelsea wanted to borrow money for a big trip to Hawaii. But instead of lending the money, her folks helped her find a summer job on the islands that paid her way over as well.

Make sure your will is up to date.

What does your will have to do with loaning your adult kids money? Nothing. But having a will helps them see that you have plans for the future. That might help them understand why you are doing what you're doing now.

"A good man leaves an inheritance to his children's children, and the wealth of the sinner is stored up for the righteous."[2]

You can write out a will on a scrap of paper, but chances are it will never hold up in court. Each state has particular requirements (such as how many witnesses must sign a will), and seldom does a scribbled note meet the requirements.

If you ignore the whole matter, some judge will arbitrarily decide who gets great-grandmother's hutch that came around the Horn in 1849.

You could use one of several computerized will-making programs. Some of these have been carefully adapted to meet individual state requirements. These can be sufficient in most states if you follow the exact details of the program. The safest course is to have an attorney prepare your will. If you consider the happiness and harmony of your children and your children's children, then it becomes a sensible investment.

Whichever way you proceed, the following are some things you should remember to include even in a simple will:

- Your full legal name, state, country of residence, social security number; the same data for your spouse.
- Whom you want to inherit your property, listing full legal names, state, countries of residence, even their social security numbers if available.

- Clear identification of the particular items you want each person to receive (e.g., "The eight-foot brown leather couch goes to Conway Charles Crighton, III").
- The debts you wish to cancel (e.g., "Upon my death I choose to forgive the balance of the $35,000 loan made on April 7, 1989, to Corral Carolissa Crighton").
- Persons to care for your minor (under age 18) children, if this should become necessary (e.g., "I appoint Conway Charles Crighton, III, as guardian of my minor children"). For many young families, this is the prime reason to hurry and secure a proper will!
- Whether you choose to establish a trust for property left to your children, to be held for them, say, until they are 18 or 21.
- A trustee to administer the trust account until the child reaches the predetermined age.
- Who will administer your estate (i.e., your personal representative).
- How your personal representative should pay your debts and taxes, if there be any due.[4]
- The amount you would like to give to your local church or other ministry or mission.

No doubt there are many other items that your attorney can recommend to you, but this will give you some ideas.

Now, some may say, "But we don't really have anything. We don't need a will."

Joel Millan died of cancer in January, and his wife followed him in November. After a lifetime of working in the fields, all they had to show was a 12-foot travel trailer they called home and a 20-year-old automobile.

Having lost close contact with both of their grown children (who lived 2,000 miles away and never came to visit their ailing parents), the Millans chose to leave their meager little estate to a local church whose members had befriended them.

They even scraped together enough money to have an attorney draw up the simple will. Upon their death, however, the children appeared and took possession of the Millans' belongings, including the original copy of the will. In fact, the brother and sister began to argue over who would get the trailer and who would get the car.

I spoke to the lawyer about what our church should do since we didn't want to be involved in a lawsuit over the matter. "Just bow out and forget it," he advised. "The smaller the estate, the more bitter the battle."

Whatever you have, try not to let it be a cause of

bitterness to the next generation.

Review your will every three years or so, and make changes if necessary. Your possessions may change, your family may grow, so the circumstances may need to be modified.

Understand and uphold a biblical view of money. When your adult children question why you handle your finances the way you do or when they seek advice for how they should establish their own family finances, you need to be ready with more than a hunch or a theory.

Following solid biblical principles helps remove your policies from being subjective and helps establish them upon something more solid than present circumstances and momentary disasters.

Greed destroys more than the bank account. "For the love of money is a root of all sorts of evil."[5]

If the newspaper account had been fiction, it would have made a great comedy. A Mr. Timmons had talked to a car dealer about a new minivan. He went home to check out the details with his wife. Along the way, he stopped by to see his neighbor, Mr. Somas, and told him about the great deal.

In less than an hour, Timmons was shocked to see "his" minivan roll up in his neighbor's drive. Somas had hurried down to the dealer and closed the sale for himself.

Furious at his neighbor, Timmons backed his old pickup through the fence and into the fender of Somas's new minivan. At that point, Somas got in his now bashed-in van and spun across the Timmons's front yard, flinging out daffodils and uprooting a prize spruce seedling. Timmons countered with a shotgun blast that took out the rear tires and the back window, permanently planting the fought-over minivan as a yard ornament.

Mrs. Somas, watching from her kitchen, ran in fury through the hole in the fence and chucked a cast-iron frying pan with stir-fry chicken still sizzling in it through the Timmons's plate glass window into their living room. Mrs. Timmons took out after Mrs. Somas with a baseball bat just as the police arrived.

All four were arrested and taken to the police station.

I never read any follow-up story, but I've wondered just what their neighborhood is like these days.

Money . . . possessions . . . greed . . . they affect more than our checkbook. They can pervert the way we look at life, God, and others.

Continual anxiety about money destroys your trust in God.

"Let your character be free from the love of money, being content with what you have; for He

Himself has said, 'I will never desert you, nor will I ever forsake you.'"[6]

The late-night call at the Lewis home was filled with joy and much anxiety. The Lewises' son, Dirk, called to say that his wife, Kim, had delivered a beautiful baby girl, the first child and first grandchild. But she was born five weeks early, and there were going to be some extended hospital costs.

"Dad, I just don't think the insurance is going to cover much of this!" Dirk groaned.

"Don't worry. Your mother and I will figure out something," Mr. Lewis assured him. He hung up the phone and explained the situation to his wife.

"But," she reminded him, "we don't have any way to help! We're mortgaged to the limit just to get our new business going."

"Yeah, well," Mr. Lewis responded, "somehow we'll pay off that bill. The hospital won't need any money for a couple weeks. Maybe the Lord will help us figure it out by then."

Ten days passed quickly with lots of family time and visits to the incubator in the maternity ward of the hospital. But no insight into how to cover the costs surfaced.

Friday was the day to check out and make financial arrangements. Neither Martin Lewis nor his son, Dirk, had any idea what they would tell the accounts receivable department.

On Wednesday, Martin Lewis opened his mail and was shocked to find a check for $5,000. It came from George Jameson, a former neighbor. Eight years before, when Jameson lived next door and had just been laid off from his factory job, Martin Lewis had walked over one night and plopped down a check.

"George, I know this is going to be a tough winter for you and the family. Well, we just got a little inheritance money, and I thought you could use it better than I could. Pay me back whenever you can."

George Jameson was stunned to find a check for $10,000 inside.

There was no contract.

No interest.

Not even a shake of the hands.

Just a nod and a smile.

Later, Martin Lewis worried that it was a completely foolish thing to do. The Jamesons moved to another town, and contact slowed down to just a Christmas card.

Then, out of the blue came a check repaying half the loan and a note: "Martin, we've never, not for a week, forgotten your generosity. Should have the other half to you by the first of the year!" The Lewises were ecstatic. The hospital was quite happy, too.

That was 12 years ago. No one in the Lewis family has been too uptight about finances ever since. They deeply trust in the Lord to provide.

The secret is learning to be content in your present situation.

"Not that I speak from want; for I have learned to be content in whatever circumstances I am. I know how to get along with humble means, and I also know how to live in prosperity."[7]

You don't have to be rich to give your adult children lessons concerning financial matters.

To say their home was modest would be an understatement. One bedroom, a tiny bath, a small living room, and a kitchen that just had room for the table and stove and refrigerator. And a front porch on which to sit for a spell in the evenings.

That's all Milt and Reba had. That, and three children and seven grandchildren, all of whom lived within a 20-mile radius and seemed to like nothing better than to congregate at their home on Sunday afternoons. The house and yard were a zoo, but no one complained.

At Christmas, the grandkids' presents were always handmade by Grandpa and Grandma. Nothing flashy. Nothing current. Nothing faddish.

Of course, Grandpa Milt's and Grandma Reba's gifts always seemed to last long after others were gone. Those gifts were the ones put in a box when the children grew out of them. They were the ones that got packed to the new home when the grand-kids got married.

For 23 years after retirement, Milt and Reba lived in that little bungalow and survived on his social security check. He never had more than $20 in his wallet, never more than a couple hundred in the bank. But they taught their children and their children's children more about the proper use of finances than any graduate program in economics could have.

There's a lot more to money than just getting more of it. And there's more to family life than trying to take care of every monetary need your adult children might have. Parents are not the cavalry ready to rescue adult children from every financial pinch. Our kids are out on their own. They need to learn to pay their way, budget their funds, live within their means.

But at the same time, why in the world have we worked so hard for so long if we can't enjoy using part of our resources to help out our own kids? Long days, overtime, and tedious hours can be forgotten in an instant when we see the delight, relief, and joy in the faces of our children—even if the children are adults.

CHAPTER 6

Saying No to Your Adult Children

Without Slamming the Door

TAL AND LENNAE LIVED ON THE CORNER OF 4TH AND Sycamore for the first 15 years of marriage. They lived in a little pre-World War II bungalow. Then about the time the kids hit junior high, they built a nice house up on the rim on the south side of the city.

After years of scrimping and saving, it was a dream come true. The kids had plenty of room for friends and parties, and they all had space to just relax.

The kids are grown now, and the house is often quiet; Lennae calls it peaceful. The bedrooms stay nice and neat most of the time; Lennae calls it orderly. And there's still room for the whole gang when they bring their families for a visit.

Their daughter, Shana, is 28 and expecting her third child. She, her husband, and their girls live in a little bungalow down on—you guessed it—4th Street.

But the two-bedroom place is quickly getting cramped, and they aren't sure where to put the new baby. They definitely need a larger home. They could probably sell the bungalow, but they have only enough equity to buy a slightly larger tract house in a tough neighborhood on the lower side of town.

For months Shana has been anxious over what to do. Finally she came upon a simply marvelous solution: "Since you and Dad like to travel more and more and don't want to spend all your time taking care of such a big place, why don't you guys move into the bungalow, and we'll move up here? This would be such a great place to raise the kids!"

That's an easy no, you say. But not if Shana were your daughter. Not if Shelli, Stephanie, and baby number three were your grandchildren!

"What about it, Mom and Dad? Will you trade houses?"

"Mom, will you keep the kids this weekend?"

"Dad, can I borrow $4,000 for a new motorcycle?"

"Daddy, can't you get Larry a job at your office?"

"Mom, you don't suppose you could fly to

Moose Jaw and take care of Lisa and the kids during hunting season, could you?"

We all have times when we just have to say no. Some decisions are quite simple. Many are not.

Four Important Things to Do Before You Give Your Answer

Listen

Make sure you've heard the whole story. The initial request might sound like this: "Mom? It's me. Listen, I know it's noon Friday, but something's come up, and I really need you to keep the kids for the weekend."

To which you might stammer and reply, "Oh, Honey, this is Daddy's weekend to rebuild the deck. He'll have boards and nails and stain all over the place. Why don't we make it next weekend instead? Is it really that special?"

"Mom, Wayne and I want to go to the boat races in Seattle because—"

"Boat races?" you interrupt. (You think, *They decide two hours before they leave that they're going to the races and don't want to take the kids? She could have called me weeks ago!*)

"Oh, it's okay, Mom," she sighs. "I'll talk to you later. Bye."

But that wasn't the whole story. Before sounding discouraging (or even encouraging), what if you pressed your daughter into a little more explanation about the upcoming races?

"Well . . . it's not just the races. Brad and Carrie Robinson will be there—you know, Wayne's best friend in college? Brad's about the only Christian man that Wayne's really close to, and, well, to tell you the truth, we've been going through some really tough times in our marriage. I mean, it's nothing we can't fix.

"But Brad and Carrie have been traveling around the area putting on marriage seminars; they know how to talk to people. Wayne just got a call from Brad this morning, and Brad invited us to come over. Wayne said it would be all right to take the kids, but I figured if we wanted to do any serious talking we had better go by ourselves.

"Anyway, I don't want you and Daddy to worry. This is just something we need to work out, and I thought maybe Brad and Carrie were the ones to help us."

Suddenly the whole request takes on a different importance. Maybe rebuilding the deck can wait one more week . . . or month . . . or year. Take time to really listen to the whole story.

Think

For you who say this is all too obvious, I can only report that most decisions are made without thinking. And thinking takes time.

Ask, "How much time do I have to think about this before you need an answer?" Up to some obvious limits, the more time spent considering a situation, the better the decision will be.

Let's say your married daughter, Martee, calls and says, "Mom, the contractors won't have the house finished until the middle of January, and the people buying this place want to move in by the first of November. Do you think that Devin, I, and the kids could camp out with you and Dad until they finish the house? We could rent one of those storage places for the furniture."

You have three options:

1. You could instantly say, "Yes!"
2. You could blurt out, "What? You must be kidding!"
3. You could reply, "Wow, that does put you guys in a bind. Listen, let me talk to your Dad about it. When do you need to know?"

The third option is almost always the wisest. It gives you some time to discuss it with your mate and to consider all the ramifications. For instance, this might be the year your son, Kory, and his family will be flying in from Maine and spending two weeks during Christmas with you. And try as you may, you just could not put three families in your home.

On the other hand, maybe this is the year you and your mate are flying to Maine for a couple weeks to be with Kory and his family. In that case, the home would be vacant anyway.

Maybe you've been telling the kids for six months that they will never get the house done in time, and that they will have to make plans for intermediate housing, and yet they waited until the last moment and then popped this on you. Or maybe every time you spend extensive time with Martee, you end up in arguments about how to care for the children. Or maybe you've been wanting a way to get to know your son-in-law better.

Think about it.

Take all the time allowed.

You'll have a better shot at making a good decision.

Discuss

Talk over the situation carefully with your mate. The best answer will convince both of you.

Miles was always a pushover for his daughter, Shandi. When she was six and wanted that five-foot, $100 stuffed bear, he worked overtime for a week to afford it.

When she was 17 and insisted on a $650 designer original prom dress, Miles sold his golf clubs and bought her the dress. When Shandi got married, she wanted a deluxe affair, so Miles mort-gaged the house for another $10,000 and gave her the wedding.

Now, Shandi feels cramped in her marriage. She told her dad she needs some breathing room to sort things out. She asked him if he would rent her a condo at Malibu for six months while she "gets her head on straight."

While Miles was trying to figure out the finances, his wife, Dee, was livid. "You've spoiled that girl for almost 30 years! It's time you force her to grow up and act responsible!"

Absolutely no decision should be made until Miles and Dee come to agreement about parenting their adult child. There need to be hours of discussion.

Pray

There is higher knowledge.

There is divine wisdom.

There is a response that will work for the eternal good of all parties involved.

But you'll never find it unless you take time to talk to God.

- Confess your own limitations in knowing what to do. "Because the foolishness of God is wiser than men, and the weakness of God is stronger than men."[1]

- Ask God for the wisdom needed to make the right decision. "But if any of you lacks wisdom, let him ask of God, who gives to all men generously and without reproach, and it will be given to him."[2]
- Expect an answer that brings harmony to you and to your mate. "For God is not a God of confusion but of peace."[3]

When your heart tells you one thing and your mind tells you something else, let your spirit cast the deciding vote. Your decision, whether yes or no, should be one that you feel at ease with in the presence of God. If you find yourself continually needing to justify your answer before Him, then you are not listening to your spirit.

Mac and Twila had two weeks to make a decision about whether they could afford to give financial help to their adult son who wanted to quit work and return to college for an advanced degree. Their plan was to pray about the matter separately every morning and pray about it together every evening for the two weeks. During the evening session, they made two columns on a notepad. The first column was labeled "Reasons we should help Darrell," and the second "Reasons we should not help Darrell."

At the end of the two weeks, they laid the

reasons before God. They felt there was only one thing they could do. And with divine approval, they did it.

Only after you've completed these four steps—*listening, thinking, discussing,* and *praying*—are you really prepared to answer your adult children. Telling them yes is a delight, and you need no practice at that. But what if you are convinced that this is a time to tell them no?

Six Characteristics of a Nice No

Be Reasonable

Your answer should come with good reasons to support it, and it should be open to reasonable questions.[4]

"We decided maybe it wouldn't be a good idea to have all three grandchildren spend the entire summer with us at the beach house. There's only one guest room, you know, and that means at least one of them would be sleeping on the floor for eight weeks.

"Also, Dad's got that golf tournament during the first week in August, and he's the chairman this year. That will mean meetings and planning almost all of July. I'm sure Debbi, being 16, will want to spend every day at the beach, but I can't hike down those cliffs the way I used to.

"But we would be delighted to have each of

them come spend a week with us, one at a time, like we've done before. The last week in June and the last three weeks of August would be best.

"Does all this make sense? We were thrilled to think the kids would want to spend that much time with us. Thanks for asking. It made our day. Call us if you have any more insight into the situation."

Reasonable does not necessarily mean that your children will agree with the reasons.

Reasonable does not mean you are always right.

Reasonable does not remove your ability to change your mind.

Reasonable means you've thought it over carefully and acted upon your best wisdom at that particular moment.

Be Gentle

A gentle no is one that will probably not anger your children. It has the feeling of tenderness and compassion.

"A gentle answer turns away wrath, but a harsh word stirs up anger. The tongue of the wise makes knowledge acceptable, but the mouth of fools spouts folly."[5]

When your son, Richard, calls to borrow the new motor home for a trip with six buddies to the Daytona 500, you might need to practice a little gentleness in your response.

You could simply shout, "What? After you trashed our camper in Sturgis, South Dakota, last year? Let them spill their food in someone else's motor home! Until you demonstrate more responsibility with other people's possessions, we won't let you borrow a horseshoe, let alone a motor home!"

Yeah, you could answer that way. And lots of times, it might be exactly what you want to say.

But you can't.

It wouldn't be gentle.

And only a gentle answer turns away wrath.

"You know, Richard, if we still owned that old camper, it would be great for you to take. But the new motor home is sort of an investment for our retirement, and we've decided to be careful about how many miles we put on it before we retire. We figure we'll just baby it for a few years. That way we won't be needing to buy another for quite a while.

"Listen, you know Motor City down on 16th? They rent motor homes. You and your friends ought to chip in and rent one. You could probably find one that fits you guys better than ours anyway. Have fun at the races. It sounds like an exciting time to be in Daytona."

For some of us, saying no in a gentle way is a long, tough lesson. But it can't be avoided.

Be Distinct

Jesus once said, "Let your statement be, 'Yes, yes' or 'No, no'; and anything beyond these is of evil."[6]

Strong words!

In the original language, the verse could be translated, "Anything beyond these is of the evil one"—that is, from the devil himself. Purposely indistinct answers are demonic.

Make your yes indisputable.

Make your no crystal clear.

Here's the way it too often goes: "Mom, can you keep the kids overnight next Thursday? Delbert and I have a banquet to attend in Fresno, and we won't be in until really late."

You respond, "Oh, well . . . we were thinking about driving up to Three Rivers to see Harold and Lucy, but I suppose we could . . . you know . . . go some other time. Or maybe we could take the kids. Of course, Lani does get car sick on those mountain roads, doesn't she? But if we left early and drove slowly maybe we could stop and . . ."

"That's all right, Mom," your daughter interrupts. "I'll scramble for a sitter."

"No need for that. Well . . . of course . . . if you want to, but I'm sure we could work something out. You just don't hesitate to give me a call . . . you know . . . if you can't find someone else."

What did you say?

Did you say yes?

Or did you say no?

Your daughter and your grandchildren deserve a clearer answer than that.

Be Edifying

Paul said, "Let no unwholesome word proceed from your mouth, but only such a word as is good for edification according to the need of the moment, that it may give grace to those who hear."[7]

Edification means that your words helped another person's moral, intellectual, or spiritual improvement. Here's the twist. We need to stop and consider how your saying no to your adult children helps them understand you, themselves, or God better.

"Dad? Remember you said you'd help me change the fixture and recaulk the tub whenever I bought the materials? Well, I picked everything up at the mall, and I wondered if you could come over after supper tonight and get that stuff taken care of?"

"No, not tonight. But how about Monday evening? You know how I like to get up by 4:00 A.M. on Sunday mornings and finish my sermon preparation? Well, I've just about quit doing anything past 9:00 P.M. on Saturdays. Can't afford to miss all that sleep."

"No" is a distinct answer.

"Not tonight, but how about Monday evening?" is a gentle answer.

This is a distinct, gentle answer that enlightens Junior about why you do things the way you do.

Your newlywed son may ask: "Mom, Tachana just doesn't like this campus housing. I know it was included in my scholarship package, but we were wondering if we could move into your guest room and stay with you and Dad until I finish law school. You guys have such a great place!"

You could just say no. Or you could say, "No, but your dad and I will help you find a better place."

Maybe you should say, "No, Honey. We really feel God knew what He was talking about when He said, 'For this cause a man shall leave his father and his mother, and shall cleave to his wife; and they shall become one flesh.'[8] It might be kind of hard to understand, but you two need to tough this out on your own." Now, that's an answer that edifies.

Be Peaceful and Strengthening

The Bible states that we should "pursue the things which make for peace and the building up of one another."[9] But *no* is such a pessimistic word. How can it ever be used to strengthen a relationship, a person, or a family?

"My daughter will throw an adult tantrum if I

tell her no. There's nothing peaceful about that!"

Remember that peace and strength are much more than just the absence of conflict. *Peace* is that confident assurance that God is still in control in the midst of conflict. *Strength* is the ability to endure a tough situation and come out of it tougher than you were before. Both characteristics assume conflict and trial.

From the time your children are born, you begin protecting them from rough times. As much as your ability and resources allow, you provide them with warmth, security, food, shelter, and love. You try to control their environment completely.

You visited nine preschools before selecting Pine Ridge Learning Center.

You talked for an hour and a half to Mrs. Miller about her first-grade teaching style before leaving Melissa with her.

You let Melissa know that 12-year-old girls do not don two-piece bathing suits and hike alone to the river for a swim.

You told her you didn't care if everyone in the entire senior class was going to Las Vegas for a graduation party, she certainly was not.

And you informed her with great clarity that that particular word shouted out in rage and disgust would never, ever be spoken in your presence again.

As you look back on all of those scenes, you are reminded that sometimes you were too strict—sometimes you were too lenient. You hope that you are doing all of this to keep them out of the trials, temptations, and heartbreaking struggles of life. But—what about the adult child?

"They're on their own," you may insist. "We don't have to make those kinds of decisions any-more." Not until you're asked, that is. Then, once more, our words seem to influence our children's present life.

There are times when saying yes would ensure smooth sailing in the immediate future. *And*, you might subconsciously reason, *they would owe me a favor.*

But some situations demand that you ask, "Have I taught them how to handle the real world of suffering, conflict, and disappointment?"

It's not too late to teach them. Sometimes saying no is just what our children need to toughen them up. In facing up to the dilemma, they can find peace and strength.

Doug was sure that he had a hot tip. A fellow at work had invested in precious metals and kept insisting that it was the way to make a quick profit.

"Look at the way prices are spiraling. Buy now, and in six months a guy could almost double his money." So Doug borrowed $3,000 against his charge card, and he purchased silver at a "bargain rate" of only $9.50 per ounce. Two months later, silver was at $12.50 and Doug was scouting around for cash to buy more.

When he asked his dad, Ray, for a loan, Doug was surprised to be turned down. "Son," Ray informed him, "if silver was such a sure thing, I'd invest money myself. Don't speculate beyond your means. You might not get rich quick, but you won't get poor quick either."

Before six months passed, the silver price collapsed to $4.00 an ounce, and it hasn't changed much for the last eight years.

Doug found himself with a $3,000 debt at 19.5 percent interest and only $1,200 worth of silver. Doug again visited his dad. But Ray's answer was the same.

"Some lessons you've just got to learn on your own," he replied. "You could sell what silver you have and reduce the credit-card debt. Then just pay it off as you can and minimize the loss. Or you could sell one of your cars and pay off the bill, keep the silver in case the price goes back up, and save paying all that high interest. But that's up to you."

That is a no that strengthens, a no that offers the hope of surviving tough times.

Be Concerned About Long-term Goals

A familiar verse from the book of Proverbs says, "Train up a child in the way he should go, even when he is old he will not depart from it."[10] Proper behavior when your children are old is a long-term goal.

Are your adult children old?

Our eldest just turned 29 at the time of this writing.

That's young.

Remember when you were 29?

My goal in parenting when he was nine was that my influence in his life would lead him to be the person God wants him to be even when he's old. And my goal for him now is the same.

Long after I'm gone, I want my son to be an example to his children, his grandchildren, and his grandchildren's children. That's my goal for his life. And any decision I am allowed to have in his life now should reflect that ongoing goal.

Your son might ask, "Dad, can you and Mom watch the kids on Sundays? Staci and I have a chance to work together at a real estate place and make some big bucks on weekends."

With your ongoing goal of a family taking Sunday as a day of worship and rest, you reply, "Nope. Because at the end of your life, how much money you made when you were 32 years old won't matter at all. But how much time you spent with your family, and how much time you spent with the Lord, certainly will."

That's a good answer with a long-term goal.

Saying no to your adult child is not always an easy decision. Janet, Aaron, and I had been looking forward to the after-Christmas trip for weeks. It would be great to see our middle son, Mike, and his wife, Michelle. It would be pleasant to visit all the relatives during the holidays, and it would be nice to speak at a local church near my old hometown.

But we also looked forward to the long drive getting there. For most folks, two tough days of driving through the remote corners of eastern Oregon and northern Nevada would be a grind. But after a hectic December schedule, the three of us looked forward to the traveling as a minivacation in itself. The Suburban would be stuffed with presents for the relatives, books to sell at the church, and supplies for Aaron's birthday party, which would take place during the trip.

A few days before we planned to depart, Russell, our oldest, came to the house with an idea: "How about you guys taking Lois, Zach, and Miranda with you and dropping them off at her folks' house?"

Now, that was a reasonable request. Their home was only a short distance off the route. But our grandson, Zach, was about 20 months old, and Miranda only three months. So we would need to cram the rig to the limit with baby gear and spend 20 hours on the road in the middle of winter with some very tiny babies, leaving their daddy at home to celebrate the holidays by himself.

When it comes to those grandbabies, all I ever want to do is say yes.

But that time we said no.

Our immediate family (Janet, our 13-year-old son, Aaron, and me) needed a little break. We needed to arrive at the relatives more rested than run down.

There was nothing easy about giving the answer, and a year and a half later, it still bothers me. I still feel that it was the right thing to say, but it was a tough no.

It's the kind of thing that happens when you have to disappoint adult children.

CHAPTER 7

Dumb Decisions

Forgiving Adult Children Who Disappoint You

DARLA WANTED TO MARRY A PASTOR.

Ever since her childhood in Africa with missionary parents, she knew that she wanted to be a pastor's wife. So it was no surprise when she became engaged to a theology major while she was a junior at Bible college.

Within six days of graduation, the two were married. Darla worked hard to put Matt through seminary. During his last term she became pregnant, and their first baby boy was born only two weeks after Matt began his ministry as youth pastor of a suburban church.

In that first eight years of youth ministry, Darla and Matt were a team. Hardly a day passed when teens didn't gather at their house. They taught, camped, sang, prayed, and cried with the kids. And they found time to have five sons.

After 12 years of marriage, Matt found himself pastoring a small church in southern Arizona. The future looked secure and promising. Then one panicked, terrifying, ambulance-screaming day in April, 18-month-old Robert drowned in a hot tub that had been left uncovered.

Matt and Darla took it hard. "Surely we could have prevented it!" Darla mourned.

Months dragged by as they struggled to handle their grief and continue the ministry.

Then suddenly, Darla left.

She left Matt.

She left the ministry.

She left the four little boys.

She left the state with a ski instructor and moved into a Colorado cabin with him.

Matt was shocked.

The boys were stunned.

The church was astonished.

Friends were speechless.

And Darla's parents, then retired from mission work, were totally bewildered.

That was five years ago. Darla is living with another man now. Matt is out of ministry and trying to raise his sons. As far as anyone knows, Darla has yet to show any sign of guilt, remorse, sorrow, or grief.

Her parents? "What in the world do you say to your only daughter who has done something like this?" they ask.

Forgiveness is seldom easy. In cases such as this, it's almost impossible.

Your case might not be as drastic as Darla's parents'. Or it might be worse.

When Adult Children Fail

What do you do when adult children reject moral, social, and spiritual wisdom and choose a life that is totally unacceptable?

It's not a new problem locked in the cultural or moral demise of the 20th century. Thousands of years ago, it looked the same. In fact, Jesus literally wrote the book on how to forgive an adult child. We call it the story of the Prodigal Son. We should have labeled it the story of the Forgiving Father. It's found in Luke 15:11-32, and it can still be of help.

A good environment does not ensure perfect children.[1]

We see no indication that the prodigal's home life was anything substandard or severe. Darla's parents, like many others, question themselves continually.

"Where did we go wrong?"

"How could we have been different?"

"Is it all our fault?"

Since the time of Freud, childhood environment—and specifically parental actions or inactions—have taken the rap for almost everything. And lots of us have done a less than sterling job in raising our kids. But remember:

- There are no perfect people.[2]
- All people are responsible for their own actions.[3]
- All people (even your little darlings) are capable of totally unreasonable actions.[4]

Geoffrey and Marcia were selected by their city as Citizens of the Year in 1988. From his position as manager of the bank and hers as kindergarten teacher, they had, in their 20-plus years in the community, touched the lives of almost every family. Just the mention of their names brought a sense of honesty, stability, and credibility to any conversation.

That's why it came as a shock when the newspapers blared the story of how their son, Allen, had been arrested for embezzling $32,000 from the new car dealership where he was the accountant.

Rumors were circulated that it must have been

difficult for him to grow up in a home with such perfect parents. Some people began to wonder aloud if the pressure to perform had been too great. Even Geoff and Marcia struggled to find fault in themselves.

But Allen's problem was all his own. During college he began a secret habit of gambling—poker in the dorms, bets on sporting events, an occasional trip to the casinos.

As his income grew, so did his addiction, until he began losing more than he made. He began skimming a little at work. Finally he was caught. It should have been no more surprising than if it had happened to the son of the town drunk. Behavior does not necessarily reflect home environment.

Eventually we have to allow our adult children to make their own choices.[5]

We never hear about the sorrow in the biblical father's heart when he gives his youngest son the inheritance and allows him to run off to the city. But it's not hard to imagine.

Bruce and Amber's son, Ted, had just finished dental school when he announced over the phone, "I've got a friend that I'm moving in with while I'm doing my internship."

The friend turned out to be a woman 16 years older than Ted. She had been previously married three times, had two teenaged children, and sported a tattoo of Elvis on her shoulder.

Ted didn't ask his parents' advice. He didn't care to listen to their caution. He simply informed them that he was certainly capable of making his own decisions. He's right. No matter how lousy his decisions might be.

Adult children need to know intuitively that the door to Mom and Daddy's home is never completely shut.[6]
What made the prodigal even consider returning home and pleading for mercy? He said, in effect, "Even Dad's hired men get treated better than this!" He knew his dad was the kind of guy who treated all people fairly.

Ronnie hadn't seen his parents in 12 years. He was lucky to remember to call them once or twice a year. They just had absolutely nothing to talk about.

His folks still lived in a 100-year-old farmhouse in southern Idaho. A big time for them was to attend the soup feed at the church or the 4-H auction at the county fair.

Ronnie lived in Seattle, where he was director of an art gallery. His idea of a good time was a week in Paris or a weekend in Amsterdam.

On September 17, 1989, Ronnie, who was 34

years old at the time, called his mother and asked if he could move home. "Mom, there's no nice way to put this. I have AIDS and I'm dying. It won't be pretty, and it won't be cheap."

On July 28, 1990, Ronnie died of pneumonia in his mother's arms in the 100-year-old farmhouse in southern Idaho—a house, Ronnie found, where the door was always open.

Adult children need to know there is a longing to forgive.[7]

Jesus said that the father spotted the son returning home from a long distance. We get the idea from the story that Dad must have spent lots of time over the months or years of separation peering down the road, hoping against hope to catch a glimpse of his son.

Late-night phone calls were nothing new to Alden and Doris. It just meant Eddie was in trouble again.

Perhaps a barroom fight.

A Driving While Intoxicated (DWI).

A burglary charge.

Every time it was the same. A tearful 28-year-old would promise that this was the last time he'd ever drink.

The last time he'd ever fight.

The last time he'd ever steal.

But nobody ever believed him.

Nobody but Mom and Dad.

There were detox centers, rehab clinics, and dozens of self-help programs. Some months went really well, others extremely poorly.

Alden and Doris never allowed Eddie off the hook of personal responsibility. They didn't let him blame his problem on others, on the devil, or on a disease. In their eyes, his behavior is sin, Eddie's sin. But Alden and Doris were determined to see him through.

"Somehow, someday, he'll lick this. And when he does, we want to be around to enjoy the victory. Our friends can't figure out why we would put up with all of this. But when it's your own kid, well, it makes a difference.

"Sure we could abandon him and let him tough it out on his own. But, in this case, we can't imagine how that would help him. So, yeah, every time he says he's sorry, we believe him. Isn't that what a mother and father are supposed to do?"

Adult children need to see an open display of compassion.[8]

The prodigal's father threw his arms around him, hugged him, and kissed him even before there was any confession of sorrow. It was a very public display of love.

Whether you talk or touch or serve or visit or give gifts to show love, your adult children need a mom and dad who still love them. When little Sissy was only a child, you would correct her and then follow that correction with a hug, a kiss, a gentle touch, or soft, kind words. Big kids aren't much different.

When Heidi was 13, her mom told her about sex.

When Heidi turned 16, her father explained about boys, promiscuity, and abstinence.

When she reached 18, her mother described birth-control methods and how unreliable they could be.

At 21, Heidi flew home from college during her senior year, unmarried and pregnant. Her parents met her at the airport, and the first thing her father did was to hug her for about five minutes.

Tears flowed from all parties, and the people in the terminal stared, then hurried on to their destinations. Heidi sobbed, "I was so scared that I'd come home and you wouldn't want to hug me anymore!" Old Dad hugged her that day. And he was the first to hug her five months and three days later when the baby arrived.

No human being stays human without love. And for fallen adult children, parents are sometimes their last hope.

Adult children need explanations when they don't understand.[9]

Often, as in the case of the prodigal son, it is the adult child's sibling that has the hardest time understanding.

J. T. rented a tuxedo last month. It was for his daughter's wedding. Actually, this was Wanda's third wedding. Few family members believe it will be her last.

"She marries losers!" her sister Patti complained. "She met this guy while picking up aluminum cans along the highway! How in the world can you get all slicked up like that again and go to this wedding?" she asked her dad.

"You might be right about Wanda," he replied. "This might be another tough marriage. In that case, she'll need someone to talk to. Someone on her side. Someone to encourage her along. If I refuse to attend this wedding, I'll never be that person."

Adult children need more emphasis on the relationships than on the finances or material possessions.[10]

The prodigal's older brother expressed some fundamental concerns. Junior had squandered half the family estate, and now dad wanted to throw more money down the rat hole by staging a big party to celebrate the prodigal's return. Dad had to remind the brother that reestablishing a relationship with a child (or a sibling, for that matter) was worth more than all the money in the world.

David and Joyce looked forward to their 40th anniversary. Years ago, David had promised her a second-honeymoon Caribbean cruise.

But a few weeks before the big trip, their oldest daughter, Brenda, was rushed to the hospital after an overdose of sleeping pills. In the days that followed, they discovered that Brenda had been addicted to pills for years. The doctors warned that something needed to be done quickly.

David and Joyce decided to alter their anniversary plans. They would stay with Brenda's boys and use the trip money for Brenda to stay at a substance abuse clinic in Palm Springs.

Their youngest daughter, Rachel, was livid. "You two deserve that trip, and Brenda has no right to take it away from you! You've helped her out financially over and over again, and it just isn't fair!"

"Honey," Joyce replied, "you and Brenda and your families are much more important than any trip we might take. We've saved and saved all these years so we could do something special with our money, and there's nothing more special than our children. Besides," she grinned, "we'll just have to take that trip on our 50th anniversary."

There is easy forgiveness . . . and there is difficult forgiveness. The more serious the offense committed, the more difficult it is to forgive. The less repentant the offender, the more difficult the act of forgiveness. Therefore, if an adult child commits a horrendous crime and shows no remorse or repentance, it becomes a difficult situation for parents. Sometimes both the seriousness of the offense and the sincerity of the repentance are hard to evaluate. Moms and dads may look at things differently and not be able to understand how the other can or cannot forgive the child.

It would be good for both Mom and Dad to chart the seriousness of the offense (with one being minor and nine being major) against the amount of repentance seen (with one being sincere repentance and nine being no repentance at all) and then

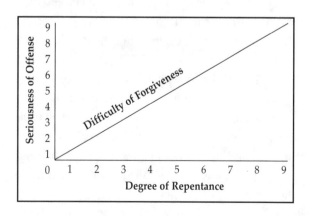

discuss the other's position before deciding how they should handle a situation with their adult child.

Truly repentant children, no matter what the acts committed, need your forgiveness almost as much as they need God's forgiveness. And true repentance of sin (that is, repentance that leads to a change in behavior) is always accepted by God.[11]

We can do no less.

But what about those tough cases where there is no repentance? We must do our share and live with the burden of incomplete relationships until they are ready to repent of their failure.

I mentioned Darla at the opening of this chapter. Her parents are caught in this very situation. To them, the offenses (adultery, fornication, child abandonment) are severe, and the repentance at this point is nonexistent.

They have made it plain to her that what she is doing is wrong in the eyes of society, in the eyes of her parents, and, more important, in the eyes of God. They have let her know, in a letter, that they will continually pray that she sees her error and changes.

Beyond that, they have forgiven. That is, they do not bring the matter up to her repeatedly; they do not talk about her failures to other people; they do not sit around allowing the situation to eat away at them.

She is welcome in their home. They call her on the phone, write her letters, stop to visit if they are in the area, and try to remain grandparents to her sons.

Often the conversation is tense, and the relationship is badly strained. But that's the sorrow of what they have to live with. They can do no more until Darla willingly repents.

Four Things Parents Cannot Do

There are four things that parents cannot do when their adult child sins.

1. Parents cannot give up.

Marti ran away from home when she was 16. Her folks finally found her in a circus camp in Florida. At age 18, she took off for Europe to sell magazine subscriptions, and she ended up in an Italian prison on a charge of transporting drugs.

When Marti was 23, she hopped on the back of a motorcycle and went to Canada with a guy who was avoiding the draft. And at age 28, she moved to a commune in Oregon and was not heard from for three years before she emerged with two children and no husband.

Through countless weeks of anger, resentment, sorrow, confusion, pain, anxiety, helplessness, and fear, her parents hung in with her. While never once approving of her lifestyle, they managed through the hurt, tears, and trials to keep their arms and their home open to her.

Marti is now 43. She's happily married and teaching school in eastern Montana. Her parents call it a miracle. You will never hear them say that their consistency had anything to do with the changes in Marti's life. But if you listen to Marti, she'll tell you.

"I tried for over 30 years to prove to them that I wasn't the little girl they thought I was. But they were so stubborn, they just wouldn't turn loose of that image. Then one day it dawned on me. They were right!"

2. Parents cannot cut off all contact.

Megan shocked her parents when she announced that she was leaving Reggie. They worked through the shock and began to rebuild their relationship.

She stunned them again when she began to date a guy with a bushy beard, a leather jacket with profanity on the back, and a long, silver motorcycle. It wasn't easy, but her parents believed they had learned to accept the situation.

Then there was a motorcycle accident. "Driving under the influence," the police reported. Megan and her boyfriend had only minor injuries. But four-year-old Phillip, who was sitting on the boyfriend's lap, was killed when run over by a truck.

Megan's boyfriend went to the county jail for a few months. And Megan? Her parents have no idea where she is. They refuse to talk to her. They refuse delivery on her letters.

That was seven years ago. "We no longer have a daughter," they claim.

They're wrong.

Their daughter, her husband, and their children just spent this past summer living in a tent in a state park campground in northern Idaho. They are hard-working but homeless, unable to save up first and last month's payment plus a cleaning deposit to rent an apartment.

"Don't you have any relatives who can help you out in a pinch?" I asked.

"Gary's folks are dead. And mine . . . well, they gave up on me years ago. They won't even say hi, let alone help us out."

With the assistance of the state of Idaho and some Christians in the area, Megan and Gary will be in a house before the cold storms of October get here.

There's a peaceful, inner satisfaction in helping folks. It's a feeling her parents will never experience. I wonder if they have any idea how cute those blond grandsons are in their green gingham shirts?

3. Parents cannot negate the sin.
If your 39-year-old son gets arrested for defrauding

the United States government with phony Defense Department contracts, you don't pat him on the head and say, "That's all right, Honey. I'm sure you did the best you could!"

If your daughter makes the headlines in the newspaper because she received her 14th traffic ticket in 10 days, you don't call her up and say, "My, the police are sure picking on you, aren't they, Sweetie?"

If your 43-year-old minister-son is accused of wife abuse, you don't say, "Knowing her, she probably drove him to it."

If your 27-year-old married son runs off to Las Vegas with his neighbor, you don't tell your friends, "Oh, boys will be boys!"

If your 33-year-old lawyer daughter is convicted of trying to bribe a judge, you can't blame it on stress, medication, or sexism.

There is right.

There is wrong.

And sometimes all of us—even the best-raised children—do wrong. And all the love, acceptance, and forgiveness in the world can't erase that fact.

4. Parents cannot reverse the damages.

When your child was four and broke the china vase, you glued it back together. When he was 17 and backed the new car into the light pole, you paid to repair both the Buick and the pole.

But when your child is 35 and has just busted up her marriage, there is nothing you can do to reverse the damage.

You can forgive her for taking the drug overdose, but you can't prevent the kidney damage that follows.

Neither can you keep him from getting fired when he cusses out his boss.

Nor can you protect your grandchildren from psychological harm when your daughter seeks a divorce.

"Do not be deceived," the Bible declares, "God is not mocked; for whatever a man sows, this he will also reap."[12]

You can, at best, help to minimize the damage, but you can't reverse the destruction.

Betty's son, Howard, was the principal at an elementary school. The school board fired him after discovering he had illegally taken $131.75 from the petty cash fund. He has long since repaid the money, and his mother has sincerely forgiven him. But that was 27 months ago, and he still hasn't found a school district that will hire him as a principal.

Sin has irreversible consequences.

Forgiveness is not the end goal when adult children fail. The prodigal son returned home to the love and forgiveness of the father, but he had spent his inheritance, and it would never be his again. The remaining share belonged solely to his brother.

The prodigal had to live the rest of his life knowing that he had disappointed his father. It was his lot to have to rethink again and again the shame of his actions. Countless times he wished he could relive the past so that he might alter the outcome. He carried a reputation in the community, perhaps to his deathbed, for being the wild, shiftless, heartless son.

It would be a while before even his forgiving father could completely trust him.

And it would be even longer before his brother would trust him again. We wish the pain ended with forgiveness, but it doesn't. Forgiveness is not the end of the story.

Remember Darla? The one who ran off and abandoned her family? Her mother wrote a note at the bottom of the Christmas card they sent us this year:

> I saw Darla right after Thanksgiving. She looks so pale and thin. I hugged her for the longest time. It's the first time we've touched each other since she left Matt and the boys. It was as if I finally realized how much she was hurting, and she finally realized how much I was hurting. It's not much. But, maybe, it's a start.

Forgiveness is not the last step in reestablishing a relationship. It's the first.

CHAPTER 8

"Well, Dad, What Do You Think I Should Do?"

Sharing Your Wisdom without Making Their Decisions

IT WASN'T AN EASY DECISION.

Our son Russ and his wife, Lois, were living and working in southern California. We had settled in northern Idaho. Twelve hundred miles is a lot of highway between oldest child and parent. So Russ and Lois came north for a vacation.

"Maybe we should just move up to Idaho," he suggested.

"We'd love to have you up here!" Janet encouraged.

"What do you think, Dad?" Russell asked.

There it was. Time for me speak with the paternal wisdom of the ages. (From early infancy on, except for a lapse during the teens, children expect

Dad to have an answer for everything.) Surely I would be able to tell them what to do with the rest of their lives. But I didn't have a clue as to what would be best for them.

My heart said, "Tell them to move! You know you can't stand having your kids live so far from home."

My head said, "It's almost impossible to find a good job up in this area, the teaching positions are already taken for next year, housing is inadequate, Lois has never lived through a severe Idaho winter, they don't have year-round softball leagues up here, there isn't a fast-food joint for 40 miles, and . . ."

So I uttered something to the effect of, "Well . . . why don't you make a list of all the reasons to move and all the reasons not to move. Then spend the next week looking at the job market and the housing that's available. At the end of two weeks, put all the facts together and make a decision. Just make sure it's unanimous. Neither of you should have any reservations."

"Yeah," Russ beamed. "That's what we should do! I knew you'd have the answer."

I did? I thought I was passing the buck. I really didn't know for sure which would be better for them.

Somehow, by the end of two weeks, they had lined up housing, Russell had landed a job, and they were making plans to move.

I certainly prayed that everything would prosper. It did.

And in the past three years, they've managed to produce two children and buy a home 75 feet from our back door.

I'm extremely relieved that it all succeeded. I wish I could have told them in the first place, "Yes, you should move to Idaho, and you will all live happily ever after."

But I didn't know that.

And besides, I can't make decisions for them anyway.

Share a little wisdom, a few stories from your own experience, and help them see all the facts. That's about all parents can do with adult children. And that's about all we should do.

How Much Advice Should You Give to Your Adult Children?

It all depends on their personalities. Adult children might fit one of seven categories.

Fiercely Independent

Lesli is 31, single, and a senior editor at a Nashville publishing company. She owns her own country home, 17 miles northwest of the city, that she shares with a house cat named Gizmo. She drives a white Oldsmobile and wears heels to work. She absolutely detests country music. Twice a month a woman named Cecilia, who speaks no English, cleans her house from top to bottom.

Most weekends Lesli hooks up the powder blue horse trailer behind her 1992 Chevy pickup and hauls a quarterhorse named Doc-B-Kind to an arena where she can practice cutting cows. She expects to make it to the non-pro finals.

No one doubts that she will. She's made a habit of reaching her goals. And she'll reach them on her own terms, thank you.

Lesli never asks her father for advice. To admit she needed his counsel would be to admit a weakness. But that doesn't mean she doesn't need his advice, and it doesn't mean he refuses to give it.

Recently her father noticed a report about transmissions overheating in pickups when they were pulling a heavy load. He worried about Lesli pulling the horse trailer all over the country. But if he called her and told her to have the transmission checked, she might be defensive and feel that he thought her incapable of taking care of herself.

Instead, he called and said, "Honey, I need a little advice. You know my neighbor, Jack? He's got a truck about like yours. Well, he heard that occasionally the transmissions overheat when pulling big loads. Since he is concerned about it, I told him you'd be the one to know if there were any problems. Have you had any difficulties like that?"

"It's the first I've heard of it, Dad. But I'll check it out and let you know."

She did.

And Dad was able to share a little wisdom with a fiercely independent child.

Sporadically Opinionated

David's son, Darren, called him for some advice about fixing the plumbing in the downstairs bath. David told him he'd need to cut out the wallboard in the hall, replace the corroded pipes, recaulk the fixtures, replace the wallboard, retape and retexture the wall, and paint it to match the surrounding room. No sweat. Darren appreciated the advice.

When riding in his son's car, David noticed an annoying hum in Darren's expensive new stereo system. He knew it could be eliminated by replacing the alternator with a more powerful one or by adding a parallel battery to boost the stereo system.

But he didn't say a word.

Darren does not take advice about stereos, ski resorts, rap music, Democrats, Russian novels, or the Cleveland Indians. He is, in his mind, an expert on those topics and would be insulted to think his father might know more about any of them.

So unless it's a matter of physical harm or unless he's asked a direct question, David does not give his son advice on those topics. Everything else in the world is fair game. Darren is sporadically opinionated. Many people are.

We cannot use our adult children's stubbornness to avoid crucial issues that must be reconciled. But we can avoid many subjects that would cause added tension while bringing no solution.

There's an old western saying that "a wink is as good as a nod to a blind mule." If the mule is blind, all the visual clues in the world will be ignored. Some adult children have blind sides. They will not accept any advice you might have in that particular area.

Save your nod.

Save your wink.

Impetuous Adventurer

DeLynne is 26 and didn't think it necessary to ask her father whether she should fly to Alaska and climb a glacier. But she did call him to ask about hospital insurance when she broke her leg and spent eight weeks in Juneau.

She called him late one night to discuss the pros and cons of leasing a condo in the heart of the city. He gave her 45 minutes of reasons why it was not the best of ideas. She ended the conversation with a sigh and a sheepish laugh. "I thought you'd probably say that. I, uh, leased the condo this afternoon," she replied.

Her father complains, "I don't know why I ever give her advice. She never listens."

But DeLynne does listen. Especially to the advice on how to get herself out of the tight squeezes that her impulsive decisions have created. His role seems to be to help minimize the damage of her impetuous adventures.

Moody Contemplator

Quin has been debating a transfer with the company that would lead him from Akron, Ohio, to Tucson, Arizona. He's been weighing it for five months.

The kids want to move; his wife doesn't think she does. They would get to buy a new home; they would have to sell their present one. He could wear short sleeves to work every day; there's a greater chance of getting skin cancer. The winters will be mild and pleasant; the summers will be 110 degrees or more. His moving expenses would be paid for; the price of homes is higher.

Two or three nights a week, Quin calls his dad in Columbus to talk about whether to relocate or not. His father exhausted his wisdom about the matter weeks ago. But he listens patiently. He knows his son. He knows that Quin will stew, worry, and be generally depressed until the last possible moment to make a decision. And then he will decide.

In the meantime, there's nothing for Dad to do but listen and wait for the decision. After that, it will be weeks of helping Quin be happy with the decision he made.

Hard-driving Perfectionist

Angie got a B+ in physical education in the first semester of the seventh grade. It was the low point in her educational career. She has never forgotten it. She dropped out of the 4-H sewing program after she received four blue ribbons but failed to take the Best of the Show award.

Her clothes closet is filled with smart-looking outfits neatly hung on hangers that are spaced three-fourths of an inch apart (she made pencil marks on the clothes bar). She has a monthly schedule that logs out in advance every moment of every day. She can tell you not only how many hours of television she will watch, and exactly which shows, but also which magazine articles she will scan during the commercials.

She is 29 and single.

As a teacher, Angie has been worried that her district might go to year-round school. "I need my summers!" she moaned to her mother. "That's when I get all the projects put together for the coming year. That's when I make up the tests and assignments and create new bulletin boards and everything!"

Angie's mother has almost given up telling her daughter to relax . . . chill out . . . take a vacation . . . kick back.

"She just can't back away from her intense quest for excellence. But she still needs me. She needs me to tell her what a great job she is doing, and how she is probably the best teacher that Jefferson ever had, and how her father—had he lived to see it—would have been so proud of her. Angie doesn't need, nor could she accept, my advice. She just needs a mental and physical hug once in a while."

Easygoing Procrastinator

Martin is clearly the best car salesman in Spokane. His sales have soared even when the market has stalled. His relaxed conversation, his ability to have time for all his customers, and his sincere interest in people more than in sales make him irresistible to most folks.

It's a good thing, too. He might spend two hours after work with a client helping him get his transmission fixed before he trades in the old gas burner, but he forgets to turn in the paperwork on the sale the next morning.

"I can't fire him," his boss moans. "He'd just get a job at my competitor's and take half the city's business over there."

When Martin's wife was pregnant with their

third child, he began to build two new bedrooms on the house. They have five kids now, but the bedrooms aren't finished yet. "February's slow. I'm going to get them done in February," he told his dad—last year.

"Dad? Do you think we ought to put the kids in that Christian school, or should we leave them in public school?" he asked one day in June.

His dad replied, "Put them in the Christian school. You'll have to get them enrolled by Friday; that's the cutoff date."

Whoa! What dad would make that kind of decision for his son? Martin's dad had listened to his son and daughter-in-law agonize over that decision for three solid years. And for three years they hadn't been able to decide, so the kids just stayed in public schools. And for three years Martin has complained about the children's education. For Martin, it's not a matter of finances. It's just a matter of decision making. Father has learned to understand Martin's personality. He tries to hold back, and he speaks out only when Martin indicates he would welcome his father's making the decision.

"I try to be real careful not to push Martin into anything he doesn't want. But those grandkids will be grown before their parents ever make a decision about school."

Timid Pilgrim

When she was seven, Chelsea wanted desperately to learn to play the piano, but she was scared to take lessons. Finally she agreed, but only if her mother would go every week and sit through the entire lesson at Mrs. McGuire's. When Chelsea was in high school, she wanted to get a job at the music store, but she sat in the car for 30 minutes trying to work up the nerve to apply. Her mother finally made her go. Chelsea got the job and loved it.

Chelsea was thrilled to get a music scholarship to a major midwestern university, but she was petrified to think about flying back to school on her own. So her mom drove her 1,600 miles and got her settled into the dorm. Upon graduation, Chelsea landed an interview with a music company in Burbank. Reluctantly, her mom flew to the coast and helped Chelsea find her way around the city.

That was eight years ago, and Chelsea's career has progressed nicely. In fact, she's been dating a great guy who's a sound engineer. She asked her mother to fly out and visit with Kurt "because he asked me to marry him, and I wanted you to, you know, talk to him again, before I make up my mind."

"Doesn't it bother him that you can't decide until I get there?" her mother asked.

"Oh, no. Kurt's really understanding. He knows how timid I am."

"Then marry him!" her mother responded. "Honey, if he'll put up with all of that, he's a jewel. I'll wait and come out for the wedding."

Tips for Difficult Decision Making

There are five things you can tell your adult children about any difficult decision they face.

1. Tell your children what you did in a similar circumstance.

Phil called his dad to ask, "What do you think about our taking a personal loan from my boss in order for us to buy that tri-level house next to the golf course? He seems to want to do it."

Phil's dad replied, "Well, that would be one way to finance it. One time right after your mother and I got married, my boss helped us buy a new car like that. It was a two-year loan. Well, after six months, right out of the blue, an old friend called me from Phoenix and offered me a great job. But I felt I had a moral obligation to my boss, and so I turned down the Phoenix offer. That's how close you came to being an Arizonian. Sometimes, I kind of regretted I didn't have the opportunity to give it a try."

2. Tell your children the facts or where to find the facts.

When your son, Larry, calls to ask your advice about the purchase of a particular automobile, you can reply:

"You know, I've never had one of those. It might be just what you guys need. But I did read in a consumer magazine that it's pretty cramped if you have more than two children. Stop by and I'll give you the article. Say, you know the Millstens? They're the new people in our Bible class. He's got one of those cars. I'll check with him on Sunday and ask if it's okay if you call him."

3. Tell your children not to do anything until they reach complete agreement with their mate.

"Man, the two of you moving back home to Atlanta would be great for your mother and me, but are you sure Rosemary really wants to? Seriously, this is the kind of thing that you have to do with no reservations. If she's not ready, just be patient. Don't drag her off somewhere she doesn't want to go, even if it's back here."

4. Tell your children to choose the option that will produce the best result in the long run.

Suppose your daughter asks, "Dad, I have a chance to work as office coordinator for a woman who's running for Congress. But it will mean dropping out of the university until the January semester. What do you think?"

"Honey . . . it's a tough choice. You have only one more year, and I know how you've been looking forward to graduation. On the other hand, you don't get an inside look into our political process very often. So put yourself about five years from now looking back. Which will you regret most—not finishing college next year or missing the job opportunity?"

5. *Tell your children to do it God's way.*

Proverbs states, "The fear of the LORD is the beginning of knowledge."[1] That's where your wisdom must begin. It's where your adult children's wisdom must begin. What God has to say about the matter is much more important than what you have to say.

Jayne's daughter, Patricia, is happily married and has two teenaged children. She worked diligently for several years, and at age 39 she completed her teaching degree. The next year, she had a delightful time teaching 27 third-grade students. Halfway though the year, however, Jayne got a disturbing phone call.

"Mom, listen, we've got a problem here. I know this sounds silly for a woman my age, but . . . I'm pregnant. It certainly wasn't something we planned. It just, well, it just happened.

"I found out Friday that I'm about six weeks along, and the baby is due at the end of September. Oh, I can make it through this year all right, but how can I sign a contract for next year? You know how difficult the other deliveries were. I'll be out for months. They'll have to hire someone else to take my place, and I'll never get back into Skyline.

"The doctor wasn't very encouraging. She said at my age I could expect even more complications. I can't believe that this is happening to me! I guess I was kind of upset at the doctor's office. Anyway, she hinted that the best thing might be for me to get an abortion.

"You know I've never even considered it before, but this has me scared. It's like throwing away all my plans and hard work. And if I'm laid up, it will be a terrific burden on Eddie and the kids. I know what you two will say, but I don't know, Mom. I just don't know."

To which Jayne replied, "Well, Honey, that sure is a tough situation. And you're right, of course. Your father and I have been pretty opinionated against abortion over the years. But you know it's not a matter of what we think that really counts. What's important is what God thinks. He's the only One who can see how this all fits together in the future, and He's the only One to whom you'll have to give account of your actions. What comes to mind are verses such as Psalm 139:13: 'For Thou didst form my inward parts; Thou didst weave me in my mother's womb.'

"Before you make any decision, I think you should read what the Bible has to say about the issue. Then you and Eddie should pray about it. I know it all looks crazy right now, but maybe there's a way the Lord can bring a solution to all of this. Don't be in a hurry to oppose God's Word."

There seem to be at least two consistent problems in giving advice to adult children: First, you and your mate may disagree, and second, your children may reject your wisdom.

What do you do when you and your mate can't agree on what advice to give? Don't give any advice at all.

Let's say your daughter, Lorraine, has asked your opinion on whether she should take the boys and separate from her husband for six months while he attempts to overcome his alcohol dependency. And let's speculate that you and your mate do not agree on what should be done.

"Well, Mom, what do you and Dad think I should do?"

"Babe, it's a difficult one. I don't think your Dad and I have ever wrestled over anything as much as this. Both options break our hearts. Try as we may, we just can't figure it out. It's just going to take more wisdom than we have. We feel like we're letting you down. Neither option seems right, and we just can't decide."

What do you do when your adult children reject

your wisdom and advice and go ahead on their own? If they rejected your advice, and the situation turns out for the better, admit your failure.

"Man, I'm glad you didn't listen to me about the job in Detroit. Chapter 13? You would have just gotten the kids settled into school and boom, the company would've folded. I'll tell you what, next time I get a job offer in another town, I'm going to ask your advice!"

What if they choose to reject your advice, go their own way, and it turns out you were right? They made a dumb decision. (See chapter 7, "Dumb Decisions.")

There's one last crucial point to remember as you share wisdom with adult children. They have some good advice for you, too. You'll be more effective as a parental counselor if you are in the habit of receiving advice.

Always consult them in their area of expertise.
If your daughter Karen is a clothes buyer for Dillard's, don't pick out your new winter outfit until she can go shopping with you.

If your daughter Kristie is a computer programmer for AT&T in Florida, she should be the first one you call when lightning knocks out the power and you think you just lost the last chapter of a book you're writing on your home computer.

If your daughter Katrina is a marriage and family counselor in Santa Fe, she should be the one you contact when your brother is having difficulty raising his adopted six-year-old.

If your daughter Kitty is in Massachusetts getting an advanced degree in theology, send her a request for wisdom on how to handle cultists who keep knocking on your front door.

Actively seek their wisdom. They might be hesitant to volunteer if they're not sure you really want to hear their opinion.

Publicly compliment them when you followed their advice and it came out right.

If the Miracle Oil she recommended took that faded spot off the fender of the car, publicly thank her for the advice.

If the value of Consolidated Turquoise Mines of Arizona jumped up 12 points in six months just as he said, let him know he's the resident stock advisor.

If the play she recommended was superb, ask her for some other suggestions.

Let them know you are going to continue to count on their advice.

Don't criticize or even joke when their advice turns out to be wrong.

Chances are they are painfully aware that they failed you, and you won't need to remind them.

Turn right around and ask them for advice another time. Let them know you appreciate their wisdom, even if they aren't perfect.

When Bill and Crystal were ready to purchase a new car, they sought the advice of their car enthusiast, Donnie. He knew just the four-door sedan for them—low maintenance, roomy, economical, good resale value. They were convinced.

The car turned out to be a lemon, and they made six trips to the dealer in the first three weeks. Donnie was embarrassed. "Dad, what can I say? I still think it's the best car on the market."

Bill believed him. Donnie was shocked when Bill turned in the lemon and bought another car of the same model. That was 12 years ago, and that car now has 211,000 miles on it and is still purring.

Allow them to reteach you the lessons you once taught them.

Twenty-seven years ago, Nick's wife died while giving birth to their first child, a son. Nick worked through the grief, later met a charming woman, and remarried. They had two more sons and raised all three boys on a shady lane in northern New Jersey. Nick rose to become president of a leading sports equipment manufacturing company.

Two sons moved into other fields, but the middle son, Jeff, followed his father's interest and worked his way up in the company as well. After 25 years with the same employer, Nick jumped at a chance to become owner of a smaller company in Florida making the same type of products.

Jeff had decided to stay in New Jersey, mainly because his wife was pregnant and expecting their first child. Twenty-four hours after Nick arrived in Florida, while the moving van was still parked out in the street, Jeff called and urged his parents to fly back to New Jersey. His wife had started labor a month early, and there were serious complications.

They arrived at the airport, drove straight to the hospital, and found that the baby was doing quite well, but Jeff's wife was dying. It was discovered later that she died from an infection left untreated due to a doctor's negligence. The family was numb with grief. At the birth of their first grandson, sorrow consumed them.

The next few weeks were a blur, but there was a funeral, and Jeff and his little son moved to Florida, where they would live with his folks, and Jeff took a position with his father's new company. Slowly, very slowly, Jeff and his mother began to regroup and go on with their lives. It was Nick who took the loss hardest.

"It's not right, Lord," he complained bitterly. "I had to go through this twice! Once for myself and once for Jeff. It's not right! No family deserves a double dose of this."

Finally, after about six months, it was Jeff who snapped his father out of it.

"Dad," he said one night with a big sigh, "I just can't stand this grief and bitterness you're carrying. All my life you told us boys that the trial of losing your first wife was the very thing the Lord used to make you the man of God you are today. Well, I want to be a man of God like you. So would you please get over this so that God can go about His work and make me the person He wants me to be?"

With a few sentences, Jeff did what no counselor had been able to do. He taught his dad a lesson that he desperately needed to relearn.

There will be many times that your adult children still need to hear your advice and wisdom.

And sometimes, you will need to hear theirs.

CHAPTER 9

"Mother, How Could You?"

Grandparenting for Lasting Results

ONCE UPON A TIME THERE WERE A GRANDMOTHER AND a grandfather who lived fairly close to their grandchildren (not real close, but not very far away, either). The grandparents were adequately young, vigorous, and healthy (not too young, but certainly not old).

These were intelligent, well-adjusted, content, peaceful, understanding, contemporary grandparents (with old-fashioned values). They had a clear sensitivity to every modern child-raising principle and adhered closely to each new theory.

Their cupboards were crammed with only nutritious foodstuffs that Grandmother creatively prepared in such a way the children eagerly ate every bite.

Having nothing else in the world to do, these grandparents often sat by the phone just waiting for an opportunity to take the baby to the doctor or the two-year-old for the weekend. Absolutely nothing in their entire house was breakable. Their Kool-Aid™ colored furniture was impervious to any stain known to children.

Their television set only received public television stations, and their neighborhood was so quiet that it was voted the safest street on the North American continent. Although they, of course, had an unlimited supply of money, they never purchased any item for their grandchildren without the written prior approval of the children's parents.

These grandparents did not have false teeth or wear strange-looking undergarments. Their favorite phrases were: "Well, your mother knows what's best for you, so we'll just do it her way" and "Would it be all right if we took care of the babies this weekend?"

Dream on.

Such folks do not exist anywhere on the face of the planet.

They never did.

Grandparents are part of the same species that includes children and grandchildren. There are no perfect representatives of any group. Sooner or later, every grandparent hears:

"You certainly didn't let me do that when I was her age!"

"Dad, how many times do I have to tell you the toys at the park are too dangerous for him?"

"Please, please, please don't feed him sweets before you bring him home!"

"It will take me three days to get her back into some regular routine after coming to your house!"

"You know I won't let them watch those kinds of programs!"

"Mother! How could you spoil them so?"

It was quite simple.

Few things bring us more pleasure in life than spoiling our grandchildren.[1] And few things will bring more tension in family life than disagreements on how to raise the children.

Since some conflict over child raising is guaranteed, it's important to build a safety zone in your relationship with your grandchild. This safety zone includes all those activities that you can do with the grandchild that will not strain your relationship with his or her parents.

You should strive to live year round in the safety zone. That way, an occasional jaunt into a controversial area will be seen as an exception, not the rule.

Jeannine appreciated the way her mother, Loretta, looked after the grandchildren. When

Jeannine dropped them off, Loretta would always ask which games, television shows, and foodstuffs were allowable. Grandma knew which parks the children were allowed to play at, which friends they could call on the phone, and which stores at the mall were acceptable. That was the safety zone. Within those limits, there were no conflicts.

Yet one day Jeannine found herself gasping, "You and Dad took them where?"

"Honey, we took the children to the Astrodome to watch a rodeo!"

"Mother! How could you? You know how inhumane and cruel those rodeos are! I would never have allowed it!" Jeannine fumed.

"I know," Loretta admitted. "But tell me the truth, have you ever been to a rodeo?"

"No," Jeannine replied, "of course not!"

"Then why don't you ask your children what it was like? Ask them who got hurt most, the animals or the cowboys? Oh, and there's a section in the program where a veterinarian explains how they care for the stock. You might want to glance at it."

Jeannine read the article. She listened to her children's enthusiastic descriptions of the day's events. The following February, it was Jeannine who took the children to the rodeo.

Loretta was treading on thin ice when she took the children to the livestock show and rodeo. But that wasn't her normal pattern; it was an exception. Most of the time she is careful to stay in the safety zone.

Fun Things Grandparents Can Do

Here are some fun things almost any grandparent can do with their grandchildren and not offend the parents.

Read classic stories to your grandchildren.

Most parents know they should be reading classic stories to their children, and they feel guilty because they just don't have the time.

Read a whole book or just one chapter per visit. Plop your 10-year-old grandchild in a chair with a big bowl of popcorn, then begin. Read books by Mark Twain, Charles Dickens, Lewis Carroll, Louisa May Alcott, Rudyard Kipling, and many other timeless favorites.

Your list of classics might be different from mine, but it doesn't matter. We agree that our lives would be duller if we had not discovered certain books as we grew up. The same is true of your grandchildren.

Take your grandchildren to historical sites and museums.

Mom and Dad take them to piano practice on Wednesdays, club program on Thursday nights, soccer practice on Saturdays, and to church and Sunday school on Sundays.

But who will take them to see the Van Gogh display that has a two-week engagement at the museum? Who will take them to Riverside Park during pioneer weekend and let them see all the folks in period costumes? Who will traipse with them to the airport and stand around two and a half hours to catch a glimpse of the president of the United States? And who will take them to the top of Lookout Mountain and explain to them the battle of Missionary Ridge?

Grandma and Grandpa. That's who.

Take your grandchildren on vacation.
Rick and Sharon take one grandchild on every summer vacation.

Tate and Lee take each grandchild on a big trip when the child turns 12.

Rudy and Maria take all eight grandchildren to the beach house for a week every August.

Hugh and Char pop the grandkids in the travel home and cruise on down the road.

Dillard and Dorothy camp out in Lassen National Forest with their grandkids and teach them a little about outdoor life.

Select whatever pattern fits your budget, accommodations, automobile, and temperament.

But for most children, any trip with someone other than Mom and Dad is a tremendous adventure. And for parents, it's often a break that offers an opportunity to strengthen other relationships.

Play the classic games with your grandchildren.

Too many moms and dads don't have the time to play games. So you can be the one to teach the children how to make winning moves in checkers, how to add points in dominoes, which direction to move the chess pieces, and the pattern of wickets in croquet.

If you have the grandchildren for the weekend, set up a card table on Friday night and begin a three-day Monopoly game. Teach them how to do a simple crossword puzzle or a complicated jigsaw. Sink their sub in Battleship, and show them how to build a fort with Lincoln Logs.

Classic toys and games don't need batteries and beeps; they need brains and imagination. It can be your privilege to teach your grandchildren to enjoy such activities.

Promote your grandchildren's creativity.

Three things that will greatly expand your grandchildren's creativity are travel, experimentation, and exposure to creative people.

Travel doesn't have to be a vacation trip. It

doesn't have to be a big deal. Just take your grand-children to explore some other part of town, drive out in the country, or look for a community event in a neighboring town.

Every time you add new sights, sounds, smells, touches, or tastes to their experience, you've given them more data from which they can create.

Help your grandchildren experiment with new things.

Buy them their first set of oil paints.

Or a musical instrument.

Or a correspondence course in photography.

Take them bowling for the first time.

Or golfing.

Or skiing.

Give them a sample of Chinese food.

Or Japanese.

Or Vietnamese.

Introduce your grandchildren to creative people, such as your neighbor (who builds exquis-ite miniature doll houses), your boss (who invent-ed a machine to locate fish), your old high school classmate (who writes novels), the guy down the street (who built a replica of the Eiffel Tower out of coathangers), your nurseryman (who hybridizes his own varieties of roses), or the teenager across the street (who writes stories for comic books).

Creativity in others inspires creativity in you and in your grandchildren.

Teach your grandchildren one of your special skills.

An 11-year-old Navajo boy sat behind a small table that was covered with beautiful sterling silver and turquoise jewelry. I thought I'd tease him a little. "These are really nice pieces. Did you make them all yourself?" I smiled.

"No, sir," he replied politely. "My grandfather made all of them, except those in the black tray. I made those."

"You really made those?" I stammered.

"Yes, sir. My grandfather is teaching me. I'm not as good as he is, yet!" His expression turned to a wide smile.

"Does your whole family make jewelry?" I asked.

"Nope. Just me and Grandfather. All the others are too busy."

That's true not only of the Navajo nation but of the entire country. Often only grandparents and grandchildren have any time for craftsmanship.

So teach your grandchildren your craft, whether it be cutting and polishing gems, quilting, writing poetry, building doghouses, gardening, bird watching, fishing, barrel racing, gourmet cooking, brick laying, small engine repair, operating amateur radio, or playing the harmonica.

Plan an activity that involves your grandchildren's other grandparents.

It's often tough to schedule. You live 600 miles from the other grandparents (or is it 6,000?). But it can still be done.

Bob's parents live on a ranch near Sisters, Oregon. Anita's parents live in Muskegon, Michigan. They get out to Portland about once a year to see their daughter and her family. But one day each year out of their stay is what Anita's parents call Grandparents' Day. They scoop up the grandkids, leave Bob and Anita by themselves, and drive out to the farm to see Bob's folks.

Four little grandsons and four grandparents. It's a pretty good ratio. "We just want to make sure the boys see us all as one big family," they reported. For the boys, it has become one of the most anticipated days of the year.

Teach your grandchildren how to do some special chores around the house.

No mother ever complained because Grandma taught her granddaughter how to iron her own blouse. The same chore around home would be a boring ordeal, but at Grandma's it's an adventure.

If you can remember how, teach your granddaughter and your grandson how to bake a cake from scratch. Show how to polish the silver, dust the bookshelves, use a plunger to unclog the toilet, clean miniblinds, mow the lawn, split firewood, operate the washer and dryer, change a flat tire, replace the light bulbs in the chandelier, balance a checkbook, program the timer on the VCR (oops! the grandkids will have to teach you this one).

If "nobody cooks as good as Grandma," it's because Grandma never taught anyone to follow in her steps. From time to time, teach the grandkids some special home skills.

Help your grandchildren memorize the names of all the relatives.

Pictures line your walls, fill the albums, and are squirreled away in shoe boxes. There's the great picture of you and your dad standing in front of the old green Plymouth that was your very first car. He died before the grandkids were born, but can they recognize his picture?

Do they know that handsome young pilot was your brother who was shot down in the war? Or that the long-haired blonde with the chic ski outfit and broken leg was you at age 20? Can they tell the difference between what they looked like as babies and what their daddy looked like as a baby? Can they name all of their aunts and uncles and cousins by sight? How about their father's cousins?

It's not too difficult to motivate children to learn. "Go over there and look at grandma's pictures. If you can name 12 different people in those photos, we'll go to the dinosaur exhibit at the museum."

It will definitely surprise your children when they find out how much the grandchildren know about the family. When your daughter comes over and notices a new photo lying with some letters, she'll ask, "Who's this short man standing with Aunt Margaret?"

To which your 10-year-old granddaughter will reply, "Why, that's Uncle Milton, Aunt Margaret's new husband. You know, the one who made a replica of the Grand Canyon out of bubble gum."

Tell your grandchildren all the important Bible stories.

Don't just read your grandchildren the story of David and Goliath—describe the whole scene in detail. Show them how tall Goliath would have been and how short David was. Help them understand how much David trusted in the Lord.

While sitting next to your fireplace, tell the story of the three men in the fiery furnace. When you're fishing, tell them about Jonah and the whale. When the two of you are building something out of wood, tell them about Jesus the carpenter. When you walk next to a cemetery, tell how Jesus rose from the dead. When you watch the thunderclouds crash across the sky, tell them how it will be when the Lord returns.

Make Bible stories a relaxed, natural part of your everyday conversation. Talk about the Lord as you would your best friend. Let them eavesdrop on your informal prayers.

I was leaning back on a bench in a mall in Missouri one day, waiting for my wife to finish shopping. My cowboy hat was pulled down, and my eyes were closed. But I listened to the conversation behind me.

"Whats-ya got in the sack, Nathan?"

"A new Bible."

"Where'd ya get that?"

"My grandma."

"Well, *my* grandma has a big one on her table, and every time I go over I get to look at the pictures. Then she reads me a story from it."

"Yeah. That's what all grandmas do."

Sadly, the little boy was wrong.

Those are the kinds of things that provide you with a safety zone. If you make that your home turf, then an occasional crusade into advice on parenting will be more easily tolerated.

But even if there is some hesitancy to accept your suggestions, you can effectively share some things.

Parenting Tips for Adult Children

Here are five things you can tell your adult children about parenting, even if they won't listen to anything else:

1. Remind them to do those things that are important in the long run.

It's called perspective.

You have it.

They don't.

So . . . share it.

Your daughter is beside herself. Her 18-month-old son has not learned to walk. Her best friend's daughter began walking at 11 months. The book she read said it should happen around 12 to 14 months. She's taken the baby to two specialists, both of whom have said there's absolutely nothing wrong with the lad.

It's time for you to say, "Look, Honey, when little Daniel's five, you'll never remember when he couldn't walk. There's no race for children to develop. Each body has its own timer. Believe me, there will come days when you will wish that he had never learned to walk at all."

It's called perspective.

Or your son says, "Dad, we've changed our vacation plans. We were going to take the twins and head to Yellowstone Park. But they've been at each other lately, and I don't think I could cope with being crammed into the car with them for two weeks. I've decided to stay home and paint the house this year instead."

"Whoa!" you reply. "Forget the house. Forget the bickering. When you get to be my age, you'll never remember the summers you spent painting the house, but you'll never forget that trip to Yellowstone."

Perspective.

It's a gift to your children and grandchildren.

2. Remind them what they were like at that age.

Chances are your adult children don't have six memories about what life was like when they were five or younger. And they probably have only a few memories from the five-to-10-year-old bracket. But you have a mental file stuffed with memories of their childhood. It's up to you to remind them of their own past.

"Mom, I don't know what to do with Jeremy. He just loves cutting things with the scissors. Yesterday it was my apron, and today he cut off his shoelaces! Isn't that kind of weird? Do you think I should take him to a psychologist?"

"Well, I'll tell you what I did when you crawled behind the couch and cut two feet off the floor-length curtains."

"I did what?" your daughter gasps.

"Oh, I suppose you don't remember. I'd say you were about Jeremy's age. We had to use those cutoff curtains for two more years."

"What did you do?" your daughter pressed.

"I paddled your bottom, put you in your bed for an hour, and made it clear that you were never to use those scissors without first asking me."

"Did it work?"

"Have you cut the bottoms off any floor-length curtains lately?"

"Uh, no."

"It must have worked."

Sometimes a little personal recollection is all that you need to offer.

"Dad, I can't get Brett to practice his piano lessons. He just wants to run outside and play baseball!" your son laments.

"That reminds me of a kid I knew," you reply.

"You mean me?"

"For two years, I had to bribe you to keep on with piano. Remember? I had a deal that for every minute you practiced during the day, I'd play catch with you that night for the same amount of time."

"Oh, yeah," your son nods. "I sort of remember

that. But I just don't have the time every night to play catch."

"Neither did I," you remind him.

3. Remind them that children do grow up.

The pain and the delight of having a two-year-old does not last forever. Thirteen-year-old daughters do reach maturity, eventually.

Your daughter calls in desperation. "Can you take the kids today? I have to go to town."

"Uh, sure. What's wrong?"

"What's wrong?" she moans. "I haven't had one minute of silence from crying or whining for 12 days. I haven't talked more than six words to anyone over three feet tall for a week. I haven't put on hose, applied lipstick, or combed my hair since Sunday! I have to get out of here before I atrophy!"

Several hours later, she returns from town to pick up the kids (who, of course, were delightful for Grandma) and sighs, "Mom, I'm sorry for that outburst on the phone. I was just feeling sorry for myself. Sometimes I get so run down."

"Honey," you reply, "every mom in the world goes through that. The funny thing is those little guys grow up and you forget all about those struggles. In September, when Erin starts kindergarten, it might settle down a little. She's getting to be a big girl. How long before school starts, anyway?"

"In 47 days," your daughter reports. "She is getting big, isn't she?"

When we look back on it, it's only the days that drag on. The years always seem to fly. You can help your adult children to remember that.

4. Remind them of the joy of having children.

There will be days they forget that having children is a joy, like the day Trevor flushed Lanni's teddy bear down the toilet and the water backed out into the living room. Trevor got scared and crawled to the top shelf of the bookcase and wouldn't come down. And your daughter couldn't reach him because the ladder got run over by the garbage truck when Melinda left it out in the alley. Your daughter ran into the garage in search of a plunger and left the door open, and Lanni, age three, ran out the driveway and down the sidewalk stark naked just as the new pastor and his wife stopped by for a visit.

You know—just one of those days.

Well, sometime after Dad comes over and unplugs the toilet, you help corral Lanni, Trevor is rescued from the bookshelf, the baby's had her diaper changed, Melinda gets a bandage on her knee, most of the toys have been shoved to one side of the living room, and you're all sipping hot cups of vanilla-pecan coffee, *then* remind her about how well Trevor did in the Sunday school Christmas program.

Remind her of the thrilling day when Lanni took her first steps from the couch to the table and back. Remind her how Melinda once hollered across the supermarket to a friend, "Well, my mother is a lot prettier than any old movie star!" Remind her how the baby lifts her head and smiles every time she hears your daughter's voice.

Remind her of the joys.

5. Remind them that God has a greater investment in that child than they do.

He will not abandon them.

We all live in a scary world.

Violence in front of the pizza place.

Extortion from a gunman at the school.

A wacko with a bomb at the fast-food restaurant.

Two locks on every door.

Danger from strangers.

Danger from friends and relatives.

A breakdown of respect for authority.

Sexually transmitted diseases, drugs, alcohol.

On and on the lists goes.

No wonder some young couples are wondering if this world is a safe place to raise children. It would be a terrifying prospect if we had merely to rely on our own ability. But we can answer that son or daughter with confidence.

God knows exactly what He's doing when He brings children into our lives. "Behold, children are a gift of the LORD; the fruit of the womb is a reward."[2]

Children light up a gloomy world. And Jesus' love for children is proverbial. "Let the children alone, and do not hinder them from coming to Me; for the kingdom of heaven belongs to such as these."[3]

And it was Jesus who warned, "See that you do not despise one of these little ones, for I say to you, that their angels in heaven continually behold the face of My Father who is in heaven."[4]

A barefoot, runny-nosed two-and-a-half-year-old knocked at the back door as I was writing this. With uncombed hair and oatmeal on his sweatshirt, he was quite a sight.

He's not an orphan.

He's not a neglected child.

He's my grandson Zachary.

Within moments, our daughter-in-law, who is a terrific mom, hurried over to our house. "Is Zach here?"

"Yep!" I answered. "He's downstairs, sitting on my saddle."

"Oh!" she sighed, sounding relieved. "I was getting him out of the high chair after breakfast and going to give him a bath when the phone rang, which caused Miranda to start crying. So I grabbed her and answered the phone, but then I noticed the front door was open and Zach was gone. Man, I have to keep my eye on him every minute of the day."

That's the way it seems.

But she's wrong.

No parent on earth can watch a child of any age every moment of every day. We've got to trust the God who gave us the child in the first place.

We've got to trust him in His hands when he's two and runs off next door to Grandma's. We've got to trust him in God's hands when he's five and marches off to kindergarten. We've got to trust him in God's hands when he's 18 and flies off to fight a war. We've got to trust him in God's hands when he's 24 and getting married. It's a lifetime of trusting God.

Our grandchildren's parents need to learn that lesson.

And so do we.

CHAPTER 10

You Can Go Home Again

Reparenting the Struggling Child

MOST MEN LOOK FORWARD TO RETIREMENT.

In fact, some live for the day.

My friend Richard was one of the latter. For the last three years of his employment, he literally counted down the days until he rode his last train.

"Thirty years on the railroad is as long as anyone can possibly stick with it," he reported. "Thirty years of being on call. Thirty years of never knowing when you would roll out. Thirty years of never knowing if you'd be there for the kids' baseball games, dance recitals, or graduations. Thirty years of never knowing when you would get home. Thirty years of spending Christmas alone in Winnemucca or some other such place. Thirty years is enough for any man."

Over those years, Richard had focused his outside energies on one project: a beautiful log home on 160 acres of land he inherited from his grandfather along the banks of the North Fork of Pine Creek on the eastern slope of Black Mountain just west of Victor, Idaho. From April to December, after retirement, he and his wife would be at the cabin, and from January to March they would be at their Salt Lake City home.

He would fish, hunt, ride horseback, cut firewood, and fish some more. He dreamed of the cold, crisp air in his face, a cowboy hat on his head, and Betty by his side as she has been for 38 years.

Well, Richard retired right on schedule, with a party, some gifts, a bonus, lots of jokes, and a few good memories. There was no way he was ever going to miss working for the railroad.

But lately, he's been reconsidering.

Everything's gone wrong.

It started when their youngest son, Andy, lost his job in the oil fields near Gillette, Wyoming. The boom and bust oil business hit Gillette hard, and Andy was soon out of work and out of a home whose payments he could no longer afford.

The initial plan was clear. Andy, his wife, and their two tiny sons would live in the Salt Lake City house for a few months to get back on their feet while Richard and Betty finished building the log home in Idaho.

It was a perfect arrangement until Richard showed up at the door with his two sons, but no wife.

"Kathy's not coming," he reported.

"She doesn't want to move?" Richard asked.

"No—and she doesn't want a family anymore."

"What?" Richard gasped.

"She moved in with another guy. So I guess it's just me and the boys!"

The plan to go to the cabin suddenly shifted, and Richard and Betty felt they should stay for a while and help Andy sort things out. Three years later, the situation is the same.

Betty has become mother to two little guys, now ages five and seven. Andy can't keep a job because of a severe drinking problem, and Richard is lucky to get to the cabin three or four times a year.

He feels trapped.

"Just when I'm set to retire, I begin to raise a family again. I didn't work all those years for this. It doesn't seem fair! But I can't throw the babies out on their ears."

It's not an easy situation. And there are no effortless answers.

Reparenting an Adult Child

Set aside failures.

Two common emotions—resentment and failure—fight to possess your thoughts during times of stress.

You will feel resentment: Why is my child doing this to me? After all we did for her, she is self-centered and spoiled. She is going her merry way, and we have to pay the price.

And you will feel failure: If we had done the job right the first time, if we'd sent him to military school, if we hadn't sent him to military school, if I'd helped him with his math, if I'd been there when he needed me, if we'd insisted that he not date that girl, if we hadn't moved during his senior year, if . . . if . . . if. . . .

Depression brought on by a sense of failure or resentment will not provide an environment for resolving the present situation.

If you are driving to Phoenix and end up lost somewhere at the end of a gravel road north of Dusty, New Mexico, you can spend the next three days trying to figure out whether you made a wrong turn in Albuquerque, your spouse read the map wrong, the guy at the service station gave you the wrong advice, the government road signs were misleading, or it was just your destiny to spend the rest of your life in the Cibola National Forest.

But the smart thing is to figure out how to get back to a highway and on your way to Phoenix. You will arrive much later than expected, and you might very well miss some events in the delay, but you will get there.

At the point of being lost, blame changes nothing. So it is with your adult children. It's time to roll up your sleeves and go to work to rectify the situation. It took Richard and Betty three years to discover this.

Richard admitted, "During those first three years, we became bitter at our son, resentful of the grandkids, and critical of each other. That's when we blew the whistle and called a time out. Self-pity hadn't helped a thing."

Betty added, "We finally realized that if Andy's wife had been killed in an accident and he had some serious injuries, we would be in the same situation. But we would be a lot further along in finding a solution. So we gathered Andy and the boys, had a teary, huggy prayer session, and began again."

Set realistic goals.

Struggling children do not always move back home, but they all need to find a new direction for life. So with you and your spouse advising, help them set realistic goals.

A realistic goal is one that all of you believe is within reach. A 45-year-old son who is determined to sharpen his game with constant practice and join the Professional Golf Association tour is dreaming. A 45-year-old son who needs two more years of college to get an advanced teaching degree is setting a more realistic goal.

With Richard and Betty's exhortation, Andy set three goals for himself: he would quit drinking, he would take a nine-month vo-tech course in sheet metal work and welding, and he would be in his own home, with the boys staying at a day-care center after school, in 18 months.

It was a plan that could be measured.

Plan how to reach those goals.
Goals are not reached overnight.

Nor do they happen without plans.

If your daughter needs to get her own place, don't simply say, "Well, Darci is going to move out whenever she finds the right house."

Instead, calculate the cost of rental, lease, or purchase (include first and last months' rent, cleaning and security deposit, moving cost, or whatever). Then estimate how much your daughter can contribute per month to that fund. If it will take five months for her to save enough money, Darci can set a goal: In six months, she will be settled in her own residence.

Andy committed himself to three nights a week attending local AA meetings. He registered and paid a deposit on the vo-tech course, and he opened a savings account (with $104) that was to be the seed for housing in the future. His goal was to reach Christmas having been sober for five months, with a 3.5 GPA and $500 in the bank.

Agree how you can help.

What do you owe your adult children?

Probably nothing.

For better or worse, you raised them to adulthood. They are responsible for their own decisions before God and society. To claim that their present difficulties are the parents' fault only hinders progress.

But you do have an investment of love, and most times you will want to help your struggling adult child get reestablished. So discuss exactly what you see your role to be.

Be specific. Here are a few examples. Tell them:

- We will pray for you each day.
- We will allow you to live at home for two years (you pay for room and board, at $300 per month).
- We will pay one-half of your rent until the retraining program is completed.
- We will watch the grandchildren after school every day for one year.
- We will pay for the rehabilitation clinic.
- We will loan you money for court costs.
- We will allow you to use the old pickup until next September so you can save to buy a vehicle.

Richard and Betty had been supporting Andy and caring for the boys for three years before they finally sat down and talked through the arrangement. They agreed to pay for room and board until three months after Andy completed his vo-tech training, care for the boys while Andy was at school or working, and allow Andy to use their Jeep as transportation during this time.

Then they had a plan and a time frame in which to work.

Set specific, objective points of measurement.

Don't wait until the very end to find out if you reached your goal. You need to have a way to evaluate progress and redefine goals and roles if necessary.

Set a date (e.g., "On the first of December we will evaluate this arrangement"). And establish some performance standards for measurement.

If your child is to finish college in two years, at the end of six months he should have completed 15 or more units of credit. If he is saving to get his own place, he needs $300 (or is it $3,000?) saved by January 1.

Richard, Betty, and Andy decided to meet every Sunday night at 9:00 to evaluate how things were going. Since Andy had three basic goals (overcoming alcohol, retraining, and saving money), he gave weekly reports on all three. This lasted about three months, then he gave semimonthly reports, and finally monthly reports. Andy said that the act of reporting to his folks kept him pushing week by week, especially in those first few months.

Explain your position if goals are unmet.

Explain what your position must be if your child refuses to reach those goals—not merely fails to reach, but refuses to reach. Sometimes goals are unreachable. Sometimes circumstances truly prevent goals from being reached. Some goals are dated and lose their value with time.

Richard and Betty struggled a long time with this step. It was their most difficult decision. They decided if Andy refused to reach the goals of sobriety, job training, and independence at the end of two more years (this actually gave him a six-month grace period after his own goals), they would continue providing for the grandsons by taking them to live year-round in their Idaho home. They would rent out the Salt Lake City house (to offset extra expenses), and they would pay two months' rent on an apartment for Andy before turning him out on his own.

They never knew how Andy felt about their ultimatum. When they proposed it, he simply shrugged and nodded approval.

Fulfill your part of the arrangement.

It might mean working overtime, going back to work, giving up golf, or putting up with a backache every night from lifting the grandkids, but fulfill your part of the arrangement.

If you fail to keep your promise, you will spend the rest of your life wondering what it could have been like if you had stuck to the agreement. That's a burden too costly in stress, worry, and pain to bear.

Fishing and hunting seasons came and went while Richard and Betty spent their time in Salt Lake City, and their retirement income was taxed to the limit. Final construction of their log home was postponed, and many nights they flopped into bed exhausted from chasing the grandsons. But they kept their word.

Accept the consequences.

A good plan works better than a poor plan.

A poor plan works better than no plan.

But no plan, good or poor, always succeeds.

Maybe your adult child will suddenly get a life, straighten out his family relationships, settle down, and live happily ever after. Or he may bomb out again and again and again. Most adult children will probably end up somewhere in between.

Andy had just finished his vo-tech training and found a good job in Ogden when his wife suddenly showed up after a four-year absence and wanted to take the boys with her.

Six months of court appearances finally resolved the case, with the boys living with their mother from September to June and with their father from July to August. Andy works steadily and dates one of the bookkeepers at the plant—and he doesn't drink anymore.

And finally, five years later than they had hoped, Richard and Betty finished the log house on the North Fork of Pine Creek. And for several weeks every summer, they play host to two grandsons from Gillette, Wyoming.

"We wish we were five years younger," Richard reported. "But we'd have deep regrets if we hadn't tried to help Andy and the boys."

When Grandparents Become Parents Again

Richard and Betty found themselves, for almost five years, not only reparenting their adult child, but raising their grandchildren as well. They are absolutely delighted with their grandsons, but they had not intended to spend the decade of their sixties raising little ones.

Lots of folks are finding themselves in a similar dilemma. The increasing pressures from both parents working, the breakup of family structure, and an increasing population of retired people have caused more and more grandparents to become part- or full-time parents of their grandchildren. If you find yourself in this position, here are five things to remember:

1. Seek the best situation for your grandchildren.

Sometimes finding the best situation will take an objective view besides your own. Your pastor or a good Christian friend might help you see the whole picture.

Here are some questions to consider:

- Is it best for the grandkids, in the long run of their lives, to be with you at this time? Consider all the alternatives.
- Is there a possibility they could stay with their mother? Their father?
- Is there another relative who could actually provide a better home for them? How about the other grandparents?
- Are you looking clearly at the challenge of people your age raising children their age?

Most children think that life at Grandma and Grandpa's is the best alternative to living at home. Most of the time they're right.

But grandparents can't be a catalyst of their rejection of home life.

The scene is repeated so often it sounds like a cliché. The process goes like this: Parents divorce. Parents remarry. Children don't feel at home in the new environment. There's hostility with stepparent and stepsiblings. At some point, 14-year-old Samantha pleads, "Grandma, please, please let me come and live with you and Grandpa!"

In order to apply even more pressure, the child begins some rebellious behavior. Finally, your daughter says, "I can't do a thing with Samantha. I think I'm losing her. Could you and Dad help out?"

And of course your heart instantly wants to help.

You must take whatever action is best for Samantha. That's not always easy to discern and is often difficult to enact.

2. *Make sure you understand the scope and the length of your commitment.*

If the grandchildren are old enough to add their input, sit down with them and your adult child to discuss the length of time of this arrangement.

Ask these questions:

Will they stay with you for the summer?

For the school year?

Only on weekends?

Until your son comes back from Saudi Arabia?

Until they graduate from high school?

Until your daughter finds work and a home in Kansas City?

Make sure you know how much responsibility you are assuming. Will you be responsible for paying the bills? Are they moving all their belongings into your home? Will there be problems with the children's other parent? How will you all know if the arrangement isn't working?

3. Make sure your role is clearly defined.

Ask these questions:

Are you to act as the child's father and mother?

Do you assume legal rights as the children's guardian?

Who sets the rules for the children's behavior?

Who is in charge of the children's health care?

Who tells them whether they can get their ears pierced or go on a date or attend certain movies?

Try to select rules that you can sustain for the duration of your grandchildren's tenure. Rules can be mutually changed and amended as needs vary, but there must be a clear agreement as to who will do what.

When your two-year-old grandchild disobeys you, is it agreed that you punish the child in whatever fashion you feel is best?

How about when your 16-year-old grandchild disobeys you?

If your grandchildren are coming to live with you, it means that they have already had at least one home environment fail them. You will want to do everything possible to see that this new arrangement will not be another failure.

4. Restructure your family life as needed.

Restructure your family life so that you can raise them in a beneficial way and yet meet your own needs as well. This means changing the guest room back into a child's room. It means putting the crystal figurines back up on the top shelf. It means installing a basketball backboard on the garage. It means buying a set of those unbreakable dishes that you swore you would never use again. It means waiting to buy the new sofa. It means buying detergent by the 50-gallon pail. It means trading in the subcompact for a minivan.

Yet at the same time, you are not a 22-year-old mom or dad. While you have accepted the role of parenting, you are still Grandma and Grandpa. That means certain things in your life need to remain constant, such as your afternoon nap, your Friday golf game, or your Tuesday night Bible study.

You will have to give up some things, but others you should not and cannot give up. Your grandchildren are guests in your home. They are precious, important, God-given guests. But it is your home, and you set the rules. They need an opportunity to live their own lives.

And so do you.

5. Accept God's timing.

You need to accept God's timing in the matter as you consider your questions and doubts.

Why did this happen to us?

Why now?

We're too old.

Too tired.

Too busy.

It isn't fair!

After all the years we've worked so hard, we don't deserve this!

Deserve?

What do you and I deserve from God?

What does He owe us?

What did we do to deserve the sun to shine?

The birds to sing?

The strawberry to be filled with sweet flavor?

The love of our mate?

The comfort of our home?

The strength of our church family?

God's timing is remarkably exact. What if He didn't make a mistake in this matter? What if this is what He wants for your grandchildren's lives? What if this is the only way that He can accomplish

His best through you?

It's far different from resigning yourself to fate. It's relinquishing control of your future to the only One who has already been there. He's the One who loves you. He's the One who has the power to keep you at all times in that love. He charts your future just as loving parents plan activities for their young child. But unlike the human parents, God's timing is always perfect.

Sometimes we erect self-imposed barriers that prevent us from meeting the needs of our struggling adult children. Our own past failures often stand in the way of being any real help.

Stewart and Leslie's older daughter, Sharon, died in a tragic automobile accident when she was only a freshman in college. It devastated the whole family, but it hit Leslie the hardest.

Their younger daughter, Tammi, was just starting high school when the accident occurred. For the rest of her school years, she had to listen to how wonderful Sharon had been at everything she did.

"It seemed to me," Tammi reported, "that Sharon got more perfect in my mother's eyes as the years went along. Never once was I accepted for myself. Always there was the comparison to Sharon, and I came up short every time."

Tammi told me all of this because she is a single

mom and is caught in a horrible financial squeeze. When I suggested she contact her parents to see if they could help out, she absolutely refused.

"I wouldn't go to them and be humiliated about how something like this could never have happened to Sharon! I cannot be the daughter they wanted. But then, even the real Sharon could not have been the daughter they wanted."

Tammi is an adult who needs some parenting. What's needed in her case, and in many others like it, are parents who are willing to admit their past mistakes. These children need:

Parents willing to admit that their refusal to accept a child's mate may have contributed to the breakup of the marriage.

Parents willing to admit immoral behavior of their past.

Parents willing to admit former struggles with drug or alcohol dependency.

Parents willing to admit that anger, bitterness, or resentment ruled their lives.

Parents willing to admit that they spent years pushing their children to achieve unrealistic goals.

Parents willing to admit that they were moral, social, or spiritual failures.

Children, whether young or adult, can be a source of pride, joy, and delight. But the world is sprinkled with exceptions to that optimistic rule.

According to the Bible, children can also bring grief, shame, bitterness, and destruction (just to name a few) to their parents.

No matter how your past failures or your present circumstances seem to bar you from helping your adult children, be confident that you always have something to offer them.

The most terrifying experience is to be alone. It haunts our nights and captures our dreams. Even so, we have never, even in our most depressed moments, been totally alone.

Jesus has.

On the cross.

When our sins caused the Father to turn from His Son, He cried out, "My God, My God, why hast Thou forsaken Me?"[1]

We were born with a desperate need to connect with other people. We reach out for family, friends, neighbors, co-workers, and church family. And if we lose all those, we haunt the dark shadows of nightlife searching for a connection to other people.

That's where mothers and fathers come in.

They are there somewhere.

They care.

I am somebody, if no more than my parents' child. There are no provisions in Scripture for eliminating that connection. And there are some harsh cases where that will be the total help you can provide your adult child.

It's not an insignificant contribution.

All your children need you.

Perhaps none more than your struggling adult child.

CHAPTER 11

Passing the Torch

Sharing Faith, Traditions, and Culture

ACCORDING TO JIM TACKETT, SR., THE TRADITION started with his grandfather during the early days of the Depression. Families were struggling, kids were hungry, and celebrations were infrequent.

So old Pop Tackett, who was poor, took one of the fattest porkers, dressed it down, and pit-barbecued the entire animal in a hole he dug behind the barn. Then he invited all the neighbors for miles around, and they had a fine supper on the ground. They visited, played the fiddle, and relaxed until dawn the next day.

That was August 21, 1933. Pop officially labeled it Hog Day, and for the Tackett family it has been a holiday ever since. Every August 21, Tacketts file in from every corner of the globe, neighbors come over, and a hog is deep-pit roasted.

Pop died in 1945, and Jim's father took over the chore. Then Jim became official host and hog roaster in 1968. But last year it looked as if the tradition might die.

Jim injured himself in a tractor accident in June and was still in a cast in August. His oldest son, Jim, Jr., lives and works near Chicago, and the youngest, John, is in the Air Force, stationed in Alaska.

Hog Day was clearly in jeopardy. Reluctantly, Jim, Sr., made plans to cancel the event. Then Jim, Jr., called from Buffalo Grove.

"Dad, Nathan has been crying for three days. He just can't believe that we aren't going to Grandpa's for Hog Day. So, Penny and I have been talking, and, well, I called John and he agreed. Anyway, we're driving out four days early, and John's flying down. You'll just have to teach us how to cook that porker. It's about time we learned."

Jim, Sr., was elated.

Hog Day was saved.

"You know," Jim, Sr., told me, "I tried for 20 years to teach those boys how to dig that hole, build an oak fire, cover the coals with wet green willows, wrap the meat in burlap, and cover up the pit. But they never wanted to listen. I had to roll a $60,000 tractor on my leg before they decided to learn."

Then a wide grin swung across the tanned, leatherlike face. "I guess it was worth it, wasn't it?" he laughed.

Hog Day? Spending a week of your vacation time, traveling 1,600 miles, and working your tail off over a fire pit for a supper that you could buy for 10 bucks (or less) at any corner in America? Is it worth it?

Yep.

Because it's a time for the family to gather, to remember years and loved ones of the past. It's a time to renew acquaintances and strengthen ties with the father's and the grandfather's friends. It gives a yearly reminder of a family's solid foundation in a shifting, unpredictable society.

Every family needs a Hog Day or its equivalent in its family's culture and tradition.

But Jim Tackett, Sr., does share a common problem with many of us. How do we share culture, traditions, and faith with a generation of adult children who are busily spinning off in divergent directions?

Tips for Sharing Traditions

Here are some suggestions for passing along family traditions to your children and their offspring.

Be realistic.

You would like for the kids and grandkids to turn out just like you. You wish they would visit graves with gladiolus on Memorial Day, fly their flag on the 4th of July, and all come home for Christmas. You wish they would plant a garden so the grand-kids could learn a little about physical labor and the taste of homegrown strawberries. You wish they would take their vacations at the cabin in Wisconsin and spend two weeks in a canoe catching Northern Pike. You wish they would not only attend church each week but also Sunday school, the evening service, and midweek prayer meeting.

But you have to be realistic.

Your children have their own priorities, agendas, and opportunities. While intimately connected, they are a separate family unit. So you have to seriously consider which things are essential to carry on from one generation to the next and which are expendable. Don't be concerned about nonessentials.

Jeb stopped by to show me his new Toyota pickup. It's a sharp four-by-four with an extended cab and plenty of extras.

"It's a mighty classy rig," I told him.

"I hope it's worth it," he sighed.

"Big bucks?" I asked.

"Oh, that's not it. It's my dad. He won't speak to me."

"Because of the truck?"

"Yeah. I showed it to him last week and all he

said was, 'We always buy Fords!' He hasn't said a word to me since."

Jeb broke the family tradition. But is it an indispensable tradition? Be flexible and release the nonessentials.

What are the important traditions? Every family is different, but often the ones to hang onto involve keeping the faith alive, strengthening the family unity, and honoring those who deserve honor.

Be supportive.

Some traditions are difficult to continue because of time or financial burdens.

Phil and Marjorie rent a house in the Florida Keys and invite the whole family for a spring vacation every year. It's fun for everyone, but fewer kids and grandkids are showing up.

Paul and his family live in Dallas. Last year it cost him $1,100 to fly his gang to Florida. "We love going down, but I just can't afford it every year," he complains.

If Phil and Marjorie sincerely believe this is a tradition worth saving, they will have to subsidize some airfare.

Maybe you need to do the same. Offer to help financially, to baby-sit, or to teach them the skills needed, but be supportive.

Be truthful.

Let your children know exactly why a tradition is so important to you. Talk to them about why you think it is to their advantage, and the advantage of the grandchildren, to carry it on. "We always do it this way!" is an ineffective argument.

Stella's daughter-in-law, Nicki, balked at the idea. "It's a macabre tradition. I won't let her take Willy out there!" she insisted.

Stella has six grandchildren so far, and every time one of them turns five, she likes to take the grandchild to Silver Lawn cemetery. There they visit the grave of Stella's husband, the grandfather that none of the children ever met.

"Your dad died 15 years ago," Nicki complained to her husband. "And your mother refuses to get over it. She has to move on with her life. Letting her take the kids out there doesn't help her at all!"

Then Stella wrote her daughter-in-law a long letter explaining why the strange tradition means so much to her. She wrote,

> When Chet was in the hospital, a week or so before he died, he shared how disappointed he was that he never got to meet and know any of his grandchildren. I think it broke his heart more than anything else about having cancer. Well, one day, just to try and cheer

him up, I promised that I would bring the grandchildren out to the cemetery on their fifth birthdays and introduce them to him. It was silly. He's not out at Silver Lawn, of course. He's in heaven. But it was a promise to a dying man that loved these grandkids without ever once seeing their precious faces. In 29 years of marriage, he never once broke a promise he made to me. Not once. I can't break this promise to him.

It's a focal point to give me a chance to visit the grave, and an opportunity to tell the grandkids something about the wonderful man they'll never know. I would appreciate it if you would allow me to continue with this tradition.

Stella's daughter-in-law hasn't complained since. Now she understands the heart of the tradition. It was all she needed.

Be open.
Don't attempt to manipulate your children so that you will get your way. Frances's daughter called to say that they would not be able to drive across the state and be with her on Mother's Day.

"That's quite all right, Dear," Frances replied.

"Actually, I was thinking about calling you and telling you not to come. I'm not feeling too well, and I was afraid the children might pick up this bug I have. Besides, there's no way I could cook for all of you. Why, I don't even feel well enough to cook for myself. My neighbor said she would bring me in a little dinner on Sunday, but it doesn't matter. I can always have a bowl of cereal or something."

Frances's daughter and family showed up on Mother's Day. The thought of an illness-ravaged mom, feebly sitting in a darkened, lonely room consuming a bowl of soggy corn flakes caused them to drop other commitments and drive to Rochester.

They were surprised to see how rapidly Frances had recovered from her infirmity, and they were equally shocked to find the traditional Mother's Day dinner warming in the oven.

Frances's tactics worked this year, but it's doubtful that Frances can be "sick" every Mother's Day.

Be open in your motives.

Be understanding.

It's bound to happen even in the best of families, and even with the greatest of traditions. Traditions, like many surnames, eventually die.

Carmen's mother called her early on May 5. "Did you get Greg a large piñata?"

"Mother," Carmen sighed, "there is not a piñata

within 50 miles of us. Greg is 12 years old and has a Little League doubleheader today. Neither he nor his friends really understand the significance of Cinco de Mayo. So, we decided not to make a big deal of it. When we come down this summer, why don't you buy Greg a piñata then? I hope you and Papa will understand."

They did.

But it wasn't easy.

Traditions do die.

Traditions of Faith

When it comes to traditions of faith, you move into a much more important and deeper realm than that of culture or heritage. Sharing faith is crucial for the spiritual progress of your family and cannot be optioned off, no matter how busy or how resistant your adult children might be.

Share your testimony.

Your adult children should be able to tell their children, neighbors, and friends exactly how you came to believe in Christ. The story should be repeated around the table at holidays (Christmas, Thanksgiving, and Easter being great ones for this) so often that they have it memorized.

Write it in detail in a letter to the kids, glue a copy into the front of the family Bible, or invite your children to attend a church meeting where you are speaking, but make sure they know exactly how your commitment came about.

You cannot guarantee the spiritual commitment of your adult children or of your grandchildren, but you can guarantee that they understand how you began your life of faith.

Share your struggles.

I had just shared with one of my adult sons how a particular program I initiated at the church had failed miserably. He stared at me in amazement.

"It flopped?" he asked.

"It was horrible," I admitted.

"But I thought everything you tried worked!" he asserted.

Everything I try succeeds? How did I ever give him that idea?

Real faith includes trials, testings, troubles, and sometimes, at least for me, failure. If I haven't shared that with my adult children, I haven't passed on the real faith.

Share your spiritual growth.

Let your adult children continually see progress in your spiritual life.

"Dad, I don't remember your spending this much time in Bible study when we were young."

"Nope. But I finally got my priorities straight."

"Mom, I appreciate how you don't get so uptight when the grandkids come over for a visit."

"Yes, the Lord's really helped me to relax and enjoy them more."

"Dad, how long has it been since you busted a golf club around a tree?"

"Two years—ever since that day I finally allowed the Lord to deal with my anger."

Keep giving them a spiritual progress report. You tell them about your health, your community, and your mental condition, so tell them about your spirit as well.

Share your prayers for them.

Let your children know when you pray.

Let them know why you are praying.

Terri calls her mother in Detroit every Sunday night at 9:30. It's a ritual left over from college days, and it ensures that they keep up with each other.

"I know my folks pray specifically for me every Monday morning, so the Sunday night conversation always ends, 'Honey, how can we pray for you this week?' It's such a ritual that I think about it before I call Mom so I'll be ready to answer her. It's my folks' way of keeping a little loving spiritual pressure on me, I suppose. But to tell you the truth, sometimes I need the pressure."

Keep the spiritual pressure on.

You have that right. Perhaps, even, that obligation.

Not all adult children follow in their parents' spiritual footsteps.

On a flight to Phoenix, I sat next to a man about 30 years old. The conversation soon turned to occupations. "I write Christian books, travel around the country and speak, and pastor a church in northern Idaho," I told the man.

"You don't say?" he nodded. "My dad's a pastor. Yeah, I grew up a PK in a Baptist church. I've heard and seen it all. Left home when I was 20. Haven't been back home or to church since."

"Oh, what kind of work do you do now?" I asked.

"I run an adult bookstore in Las Vegas," he admitted.

The conversation trailed off.

I didn't think about him much on the rest of the trip, but I sure thought about his parents. Somewhere, I imagined, working hard to serve the Lord, are a mom and a dad, heartbroken over a son who chose to reject everything they cherish.

How to Handle Antireligious Adult Children

If you have antireligious adult children, there are several things to remember.

Don't ignore them.

Don't write off your children. Don't disown them. Don't reject their love for you. Don't withhold your love for them. Your love for them should not be dependent on their behavior or their beliefs. God has shown us how to do that. "But God demonstrates His own love toward us, in that while we were yet sinners, Christ died for us."[1]

I had just spent an hour and 45 minutes as a college student in a philosophy class where we debated the existence of God. The professor and 95 percent of the students raked me and two others over the coals for stubbornly holding onto our beliefs.

Complaining about unfair treatment, I walked with the professor back to his office. "Mr. Bly," he said, "you left out the strongest argument for God's existence."

"Which is?" I probed.

"The shoebox-full-of-cookies argument," he lectured. Then he led me into his office. He pulled the lid off an orange-colored shoebox and offered me a luscious chocolate chip cookie that would make Mrs. Fields jealous.

"My Christian mother sent me these," he said. "I'm 51 years old, and my mother still sends me a box of homemade cookies about once a month. You see, that's the argument you forgot. Love that never gives up. After all I've said and done over the years, there's no rational way to explain it."

Don't ignore the child. Even if he's a 51-year-old college professor.

Don't ignore the subject.

If you and your adult children disagree on matters of faith, it would be much more peaceful to dismiss any such conversation. But faith in Christ is much too important to skip over.

"Oh, I never talk to my daughter about religion, politics, or Oprah Winfrey," the lady told me.

Bad choice. If the building is burning down, tell your children about the fire. If your children are burning out their lives, warn them of the spiritual consequences. It would be adult-child neglect to do anything less.

It might mean you have to do more Bible study, take a correspondence course, or read more apologetic literature to keep up with your adult children's arguments. You don't have to be mindlessly repetitive. You don't have to nag. But you have to be prepared to say something. Peter said that we must always be "ready to make a defense to everyone who asks you to give an account for the hope that is in you, yet with gentleness and reverence."[2]

And that certainly includes adult children.

Be openly consistent in living your faith.

The atheist's most common complaint always begins, "I once knew a Christian who. . . ."

Then follows a real or imagined tale of hypocrisy and inconsistency. When the example is Mom or Dad, the wall erected is a difficult one to cross.

Neal, who is close to 80, is a model of Christian consistency to follow. He summed it up this way:

"When I first began to raise my boys, I realized that I might not be able to convince them all to follow in the faith. But I was determined to give them a good example. When they stand around my grave some day, they might not all be believers, but they are going to have to say, 'Well, the old man certainly believed in it, didn't he? Right to the very end.'"

One of the most dramatic statements about character given to us in the Old Testament concerns a little-known man named Enoch. "And Enoch walked with God; and he was not, for God took him."[3] He will forever be known simply as the person who "walked with God." Not a bad epitaph for any of us.

If You Choose to Ignore Your Adult Children

Many parents feel that they've earned the right to ignore the needs and struggles of their adult children.

"Look, I changed 10,000 smelly diapers. I was in the PTA for 31 years. I sat up 'til 1:00 A.M. every night the girls went on a date. I made cheerleading skirts until my fingers bled. I typed term papers. I drove a truck through a tornado 1,100 miles to move the kid. I flew across the country to be with them when the first child was born. I've done it all.

"Now they're on their own. They will sink or swim without us. We have retired from parenting. Our kids will get along without our help."

Well, you're probably right.

They'll get along.

Not as well, perhaps, but they will survive.

You, of course, will be poorer for it.

You'll miss the tears.

You won't hear about the miscarriage or about when he was purposely being overlooked for the promotion. Or the car wreck that took the life of her best friend. Or the sad television movie that reminded them of Grandpa. Or the crushing depression he experienced when his wife walked out and left him.

You'll miss the laughter.

You'll never hear about the time the tent blew down while they were camping at the beach. You won't know about the clerk who thought you were your son's brother, the crazy mix-up at the dry cleaners, or the woman who always calls and asks for Leon. You won't know what happened on the 10th green after the marmot carried off his golf ball or what happened at the lip-sync contest at work when she donned a blonde wig and mimicked Dolly Parton.

Sure you might miss the laughter, but look on the bright side.

You'll miss the challenge, too.

You won't have to help your children figure out how to pay the hospital bill. How to find a better-paying job. How to have that baby in August and be back on the job by September. You won't have to advise them how to cope with a rebellious teen, how to forgive an adulterous mate, how to move three kids into a two-bedroom house, or how to get your grandkid's thumb unstuck from the bathtub faucet.

You have enough challenges of your own. Why accept more from your adult children?

And you'll miss the need for endurance.

You won't have to struggle as your adult child fights off alcohol dependence. You won't have to worry daily about her abusive mate. You won't need to grow strong in faith as your kids struggle to face up to the cultists who keep knocking on their front door. You won't have to feel the strain they face when they give daily medication and treatments to their baby.

If you miss all of this, you'll also miss the victories.

The three-page accolade your son received in the trade journal will be reduced to a couple of words on the Christmas card. Since you never asked about his depression, you probably won't hear about its cure. The advanced college degree doesn't sound like much if you didn't live through your daughter's two years of all-night studies and all-day work shifts.

Sure, they will lose some.

But they will win some big ones, too.

This past season, our son's Little League team won the league championship. The parents of all 14 kids on the team were in the stands for that last game. It's the way it should be. Throughout their lives, the boys have competed to impress their parents.

But it won't be the last time those kids win.

They'll have victories when they are 16, 26, and 56. But will you be there to cheer them on?

Sure you can ignore the continuing role of parents. All it will cost you is tears, laughter, challenge, endurance, and victory.

The very things that make human life worth living.

Is continuing to parent adult children all that important?

Yep.

The position you play in your children's lives is irreplaceable.

No matter what their age.

Most of the world watched the 1992 Summer Olympic Games in Barcelona. Many of us caught the action of the men's 400-meter race. For a few moments, we forgot who won, and all of us watched, instead, British runner Derek Redmond.

He was the one who violently pulled a hamstring muscle and collapsed to the track midway through the race. With the crush of disappointment and the piercing agony of pain written on his face, he struggled to get to his feet. Olympic officials hurried to help him off the track. But with tears rolling down his face, he shoved them aside.

Suddenly all of us watching at home, and most of the people in the crowd, could see what he was doing. He was going to finish the race! Years of training, hard work, and sacrifice had disintegrated on that hot Barcelona afternoon, but he was resolved to finish the race.

The pain was so great he stumbled, hopped, and hobbled. It looked for a while as if there was no physical way he could go on. The race was long over when the crowd began to cheer for Derek. Even with their encouragement, it appeared he just couldn't do it. Terrifying pain was overcoming the will to go on.

Then an older man illegally broke through the ranks of people around the track. The man walked right up to Derek Redmond and grabbed him around the chest. Derek threw his arm over the man's shoulder.

That was no official trying to get Derek off the track. That man was trying to help a courageous, determined athlete complete the race.

The man was Derek Redmond's father.

Still in anguish, Derek completed the race to the standing ovation of all in the stadium.

A loser?

Not in my eyes.

Nor, I'm sure, in the eyes of his father.

Few of us will ever have sons or daughters who will compete in the Olympics. But it's almost assured that our children will face tough times, some as grueling as that of Derek Redmond.

Then it will be your turn.

My turn.

We'll fight our way through the crowd. We'll lift them up.

We'll let them lean on our shoulders.

And we'll help them cross their finish line.

It will be angels in heaven giving the standing ovation.

That's what parenting is all about.

No matter what the age of your child.

Notes

Chapter 1

1. Dr. James Dobson, *Hide or Seek* (Old Tappan, NJ: Revell, 1990), 110.
2. Ibid., 111.
3. Ibid., 113.
4. William Saroyan, *Sons Come & Go, Mothers Hang in Forever* (New York: McGraw-Hill, 1976).
5. Allan Schnaiberg and Sheldon Goldenberg, "From Empty Nest to Crowded Nest: The Dynamics of Incompletely-Launched Young Adults," *Social Problems*, 36:3, June 1989, 256.
6. Christopher Lasch, *Haven in a Heartless World: The Family Besieged* (New York: Basic Books, 1977).
7. William S. Aquilino and Khalil R. Supple, "Parent-Child Relations and Parents' Satisfaction with Living Arrangements When Adult Children Live at Home," *Journal of Marriage and the Family*, 53, February 1991, 14.
8. Erma Bombeck, *Lewiston Morning Tribune*, 12, September 1992, 2D.

Chapter 2

1. Frances K. Goldscheider and Calvin Goldscheider, "Family Structure and Conflict: Nest-Leaving Expectations of Young Adults and their Parents," *Journal of Marriage and the Family*, 51, February 1989, 87.
2. Schnaiberg and Goldenberg, "From Empty Nest to Crowded Nest," 231.

3. Ibid., 232.
4. Aquilino and Supple, "Parent-Child Relations," 14.
5. Proverbs 22:6.
6. See Genesis 4.
7. Aquilino and Supple, "Parent-Child Relations," 24.
8. Ibid., 24.
9. Ibid., 25.
10. Ibid., 18.
11. Ibid., 17.
12. Ibid., 25.
13. Genesis 2:24.
14. Aquilino and Supple, "Parent-Child Relations," 25.
15. See Luke 15:11-32.
16. Luke 15:20, NIV.
17. See chapter 7, "Dumb Decisions," for a complete look at the biblical story of the forgiving father.

Chapter 3
1. Parts of this chapter are adapted from Stephen A. Bly, "Plans Change," *Moody Magazine* (June 1991).
2. 1 Peter 3:7.

Chapter 4
1. Luke 10:41-42.
2. Jeremiah 9:23-24.
3. See Luke 17:3.
4. See 2 Timothy 4:2.
5. See Galatians 6:1-2.
6. See 2 Thessalonians 3:15.
7. James 3:17.
8. See Ephesians 4:29; Colossians 4:6.

Chapter 5
1. For more on agreement in parenting, see Stephen and Janet Bly, *Be Your Mate's Best Friend* (Chicago: Moody Press, 1988).
2. Proverbs 13:22.

3. For example, *Willmaker* (Nolo Press, 950 Parker St., Berkeley, CA 94710).
4. Several of the above points have been adapted from *Willmaker* (see note 3).
5. 1 Timothy 6:10.
6. Hebrews 13:5.
7. Philippians 4:11-12.

Chapter 6

1. 1 Corinthians 1:25.
2. James 1:5.
3. 1 Corinthians 14:33.
4. See James 3:17.
5. Proverbs 15:1-2.
6. Matthew 5:37.
7. Ephesians 4:29.
8. Genesis 2:24.
9. Romans 14:19.
10. Proverbs 22:6.

Chapter 7

1. See Luke 15:12-13.
2. See Romans 3:23.
3. See Ezekiel 18:4.
4. See Jeremiah 17:9.
5. See Luke 15:13.
6. See Luke 15:17-18.
7. See Luke 15:20.
8. See Luke 15:20-24.
9. See Luke 15:31-32.
10. See Luke 15:32.
11. See 1 John 1:9.
12. Galatians 6:7.

Chapter 8

1. Proverbs 1:7.

Chapter 9

1. For a detailed account on spoiling your grandkids in a good way, see Stephen and Janet Bly, *How to Be a Good Grandparent* (Chicago: Moody Press, 1990).
2. Psalm 127:3.
3. Matthew 19:14.
4. Matthew 18:10.

Chapter 10

1. Mark 15:34.

Chapter 11

1. Romans 5:8.
2. 1 Peter 3:15.
3. Genesis 5:24.

Other Books to Strengthen Your Relationships
From Focus on the Family®

Parents Guide to Top 10 Dangers Teens Face
Parents can help guard their teens against alcoholism, drug addiction, promiscuity and other reckless behaviors by reading Stephen Arterburn's *Parents Guide to Top 10 Dangers Teens Face.* Filled with proven principles, it helps parents heed the warning signs, ward off potential problems and direct their kids down the road to success. Paperback.

Give Them Wings
When kids hit their teenage years, the role of parents begins to change. In *Give Them Wings*, author Carol Kuykendall offers encouragement for raising kids to be responsible, godly men and women and for looking toward the empty nest with hope. Paperback.

Guiding Your Family in a Misguided World
With all the mixed messages society spouts, Tony Evans's *Guiding Your Family in a Misguided World* is an indispensable guide for creating a stable, Christ-centered home, developing a strong personal faith and living a life that's pleasing to God. Paperback.

• • •

9BPXMP

FOCUS ON THE FAMILY®
Welcome to the Family!

Whether you received this book as a gift, borrowed it from
a friend, or purchased it yourself, we're glad you read it!
It's just one of the many helpful, insightful, and encouraging
resources produced by Focus on the Family.

In fact, that's what Focus on the Family is all about—
providing inspiration, information, and biblically based
advice to people in all stages of life.

It began in 1977 with the vision of one man, Dr. James Dobson,
a licensed psychologist and author of 16 best-selling books on
marriage, parenting, and family. Alarmed by the societal, political,
and economic pressures that were threatening the existence
of the American family, Dr. Dobson founded Focus on the Family
with one employee—an assistant—and a once-a-week
radio broadcast, aired on only 36 stations.

Now an international organization, Focus on the Family is
dedicated to preserving Judeo-Christian values and strengthening
the family through more than 70 different ministries, including
eight separate daily radio broadcasts; television public service
announcements; 11 publications; and a steady series of
award-winning books, films, and videos for people
of all ages and interests.

Recognizing the needs of, as well as the sacrifices and important
contribution made by, such diverse groups as educators, physi-
cians, attorneys, crisis pregnancy center staff, and single parents,
Focus on the Family offers specific outreaches to uphold and minister to these individuals, too. And it's all done for one purpose,
and one purpose only: to encourage and strengthen individuals
and families through the life-changing message of Jesus Christ.

• • •

For more information about the ministry, or if we can be of help to
your family, simply write to Focus on the Family, Colorado Springs,
CO 80995 or call 1-800-A-FAMILY (1-800-232-6459). Friends in
Canada may write Focus on the Family, P.O. Box 9800, Stn.
Terminal, Vancouver, B.C. V6B 4G3 or call 1-800-661-9800. Visit our
Web site—www.family.org—to learn more about the ministry or to
find out if there is a Focus on the Family office in your country.

We'd love to hear from you!